9/22

# Conjugal Spirituality

## The Primacy of Mutual Love in Christian Tradition

Mary Anne McPherson Oliver

Sheed & Ward

Sheed & Ward™ is a service of The National Catholic Reporter Publishing Company.

---

**Library of Congress Cataloguing-in-Publication Data**

Oliver, Mary Anne McPherson, 1935-
    Conjugal spirituality : the primacy of mutual love in Christian tradition / Mary Anne McPherson Oliver.
        p.    cm.
    Includes bibliographical references and indexes.
    ISBN 1-55612-312-4  (alk. paper)
    1. Marriage—Religious aspects—Christianity. 2. Sex—Religious aspects—Christianity. 3. Celibacy—Christianity. 4. Married people—Religious life. 5. Mysticism.  I. Title.
BT706.045    1994
248.4—dc20                                              94-23306
                                                            CIP

---

Published by: Sheed & Ward
             115 E. Armour Blvd.
             P.O. Box 419492
             Kansas City, MO 64141

To order, call: (800) 333-7373

*Cover design by Emil Antonucci.*

# Contents

*To all who have helped,*
*especially Ray*

# Preface

TWENTY-ODD YEARS AGO, in the process of getting a doctorate in theology, I discovered the history of spirituality, initially in the Roman Catholic version. I read saints' writings. I read saints' lives. I plowed through Garrigou-Lagrange's long attempt to synthesize 19 centuries of Christian experience. Sometimes I would say with satisfaction, "I've seen that happen," or "So that's what that means." Sometimes I would say with interest: "How different people are," or "How times have changed." But often, quite often, I found myself puzzled, saying "Yes, but . . ." "Yes, but not quite like that," or "Yes, but that's not all," or even "That just isn't right, though I don't know why."

As books began to repeat themselves or to be variations on basic patterns, I had some sense of the essential structure of spirituality, yet my discomfort remained. I read on, thinking that Protestant writers would surely fill out the picture satisfactorily, but again I did not find what I was seeking. Finally, I turned from books to people. I talked to ministers, I talked to monks. I went on retreats, visited intentional communities, spent a whole liturgical year at Taizé, an ecumenical monastery in France. Still my reservations accumulated.

Gradually I came more and more to suspect that it was not just a matter of this or that detail, this or that theory. I began to realize that from my perspective, spirituality as recorded in writing and as taught by the churches and their representatives was lacking. It was the whole of spiritual history and theology that was warped—not untrue, but somehow slightly out of focus, for me. It finally dawned on me that for 30-odd years I had lived in one intimate partnership, a fact of tremendous significance to my being and to my spiritual life, yet the *couple* in tradition was virtually nonexistent as a theologically and spiritually significant unit. When mentioned at all, it was either quickly dissolved into its two constituent parts or assimilated into a familial or communal group. I finally came to the simple realization that spirituality as written and taught is basically celibate and/or monastic, and I am not.

Armed with this common sense discovery, I approached ministers and monks with more specificity, trying to discover in what way the couple as couple could most fully live as Christian, but the people I talked to knew only the traditional ways which I had come to realize were grounded in the particularity of the celibate experience. I revisited the literature as well, reasoning that since some very large percentage of Christians have always married, there must be at least traces of a dyadic way. And traces there were, here and there, enough to reconstitute a kind of hidden, underground current in the history of the Church, a kind of marginal, ill-defined movement which bubbles to the surface now and again, in the middle of the 20th century gaining substance and speed until now we can begin to see something of its shape and direction.

This book is an attempt to present the shape underlying those traces, so that couples may go beyond their silent mystification and finally take full and conscious part in the adventure of the spirit, finding other models than the celibate one which leaves them second-class citizens, and the intentional community which beclouds and dilutes their basic, conjugal vocation. The first chapter will lay out the evidence for my contention that spirituality, both Catholic and Protestant, is celibate, and why this is inadequate or even pernicious for couples. Others will explore the underground tradition of conjugal spirituality — former heresy, present possibility — countering both those Roman Catholics who still proceed as though individuals operate in isolation and marriage "divides the heart against God," and those Protestants who still contend that knowledge of God is not communicated in sex and that marriage is only a matter of individual journeys to spiritual growth.

One explanatory note is necessary. My interest is not in institutions, however defined, but in the fact that people can and often have coexisted in significant and sometimes lifelong relationships of the closest possible intimacy. My focus is on the spiritual significance of this fact and the spiritual potential of this human possibility.

# 1

# "Spirituality" is Celibate

I AM PROPOSING a new-old discipline to be called conjugal spirituality. It is new in that it will still not be found as a subdivision in any reference work (despite recent upgradings of the laity and the body in religious and theological circles). The closest equivalent is the listing of "Sexuality" in *The Westminster Dictionary of Christian Spirituality*, which summarizes the Biblical and historical attitudes toward sexuality and notes the modern movement toward integrative wholism, "a relatively recent development."[1] Yet it is also old in the sense that pair-bonding, though historically ignored or discounted by the theological community, has existed among Christians from the beginning. In order to clear the way for this new discipline, I will need to establish two things: first, that all the things we think of as "religion" today are in fact "celibate" practice; and second, that this "celibate spirituality," since it is shaped by a way of life subtly but surely unlike that of the great majority of people, is inadequate and in some cases even pernicious, particularly for couples.

By "celibate practice" I mean all the religious lifestyles which fully exclude sexual relating, and in which the primary responsibility is to the self and the primary relational ideal one of flexible, unattached availability. Our "celibate" spirituality comes in two basic modes which I would like to describe in some detail: the eremitic and the monastic, the one-alone-with-God, and the group-together-with-God. There are two reasons for this digression. First, from the basic elements of these two lifestyles come all the historical variations (priests, knights and hospitalers adapted eremitic and monastic practices, and the newer "active" orders from the 13th century onward made their own combination of elements, carrying their cloister around inside them, interiorized, as they worked "in the world"), as well as the "religion" we know today. A close examination of the spiritual character of the lives of the hermit and the monk will provide the means for recognizing the extent to which our historical tradition is celibate, and make modern variations on the theme more easily identifiable. And second, a significant change in spirituality occurs in passing from that solitary to that communal lifestyle, and recognition of this change will help prepare us for the similarly drastic spiritual shift which must occur in order to pass from either state to the conjugal life.

## The Hermit

The early Christian hermits traveled into trackless deserts, farther and farther in as the successive retreats became crowded. The desert was not a barren place to them but, as for their Jewish forebears, a place where one could meet God, a place of covenant renewal and purification. More than for their Jewish forebears it was a place to be united with God, to experience Pentecost and to realize the holiness of God communicated to humankind. They considered the eremitical life to be a life directly and immediately centered on the adoration of God, without dilution. Thus, they wanted to anticipate in this life the silence and peace of eternity, and to be like the angels in their constant praise.

They wanted to live anonymously, separated from the world and alone, or not alone but with God, *solus ad solum*. They took axes, quarried rock, brought logs from marshes and built cells out of sight and hearing of each other. No hermit would invade the silence of another unless that one had been missing from the weekly gathering for worship, and was therefore presumed to be sick. In these places, and with a minimum of possessions, they spent their time praying, reading, reciting the psalter, and doing what manual labor was necessary to stay alive — often plaiting palm-leaves and making baskets that could be exchanged for bread from the sacristan at church. And that was all. Even on visits and at Sunday services they were often wordless.

They wished to live out their lives in this solitude and silence, yet some of them and some of their spiritual descendants were continually being sought out for spiritual counsel and dragged forth from their desert retreats to mediate in the quarrels of the world, to govern monasteries, dioceses, and even the Church. They were thus disturbed in their retreats because they became famous as athletes of God. By focusing intensely on God in isolation from human relationships, some of them arrived at a particular kind of transformation of the person, one that is perceptible to others. The *Life of Antony* recounts that when his friends tore down the door of the deserted fort where he had barricaded himself for 20 years, he "came forth as though from some shrine, having been led into divine mysteries and inspired by God."[2] Other accounts try to describe a light or an emanation from the person, an inner quality which is somehow outwardly visible in the face.

We have some notion of what happened to these hermits in their years of solitude through their sayings and accounts of their lives by others. Living in the desert itself was difficult enough; water was hard to find. There were physical discomforts to contend with, heat and hunger, as well as the psychological ones of isolation, depression, frustration, and boredom. Yet the hardships stemming from the physical environment seemed as nothing beside the biggest trial of all — that of perseverance in prayer. Abbot Agatho, when asked what virtue in the eremitical life was the most laborious, replied, "There is no labor so great as praying to God: for when a man wishes to pray to his God, the hostile demons make haste to interrupt his prayer . . . With any other labor that a man undertakes in the life of religion, however instant and close he keeps to it, he hath some rest: but prayer hath the travail of a mighty conflict to one's last breath."[3]

And the more one persevered in prayer, the fiercer became the inner war of the will against evil. As the abbot Mathois said, "The nearer a man approaches to God, the greater sinner he sees himself to be. For the prophet Isaiah saw God, and said that he was unclean and undone."[4] The spiritual life of the hermit was a lifelong struggle to cooperate in the work of God, which is to root out our self-centeredness so that we become fit instruments, strong enough to love God and neighbor as we ought.

The dramatic nature of this great struggle and the poetic extravagance of their ambition is perhaps best illustrated in an anecdote about the abbot Joseph, who comes to abbot Lot and says to him, "Father, according to my strength I keep a modest rule of prayer and fasting and meditation and quiet, and according to my strength I purge my imagination: what more must I do?" The old man, rising, holds up his hands against the sky, and his fingers become like 10 torches of fire, and he says, "If thou wilt, thou shalt be made wholly a flame."[5]

Asceticism, the inner and outer discipline aimed at asserting control over mind and body, was only the beginning for them, not an end in itself. Fiery transformation by the spirit was their goal and the desert would be their means. The hermit shut out the world to concentrate on self and God, simplifying and intensifying until one's life could burst into flame. First came the necessary withdrawal. As one unnamed desert Father explained: "He who abides in the midst of men, because of the turbulence, he sees not his sins, but when he hath been quiet, above all in solitude, then does he recognize his own default."[6] Then there are the spiritual exercises of prayer, and persevering in prayer, and the physical exercises such as intentional fasting, nightlong vigils, "metanies" (touching the head to the ground), and self-inflicted flagellation. Gradually, over the years, illusions about God and self dissipate, the true extent of sin becomes visible, the will is then roused to combat it, and control over the self begins. The self remains always a sinner, the self does not change, but its behavior and therefore its appearance to others does. The story is told of "a certain old man" who had lived 50 years neither eating bread nor readily drinking water. He thought he had killed lust, avarice, and vainglory in himself. A wiser abbot, Abraham, shows him that since he still recognizes women, gold, and praise as desirable, the sin in him has been only subdued, not killed: "These passions live, but by holy men they are in some sort bound."[7]

Thus it was that the almost inhuman austerity of desert life brought about in some hermits such qualities of loving-kindness, magnanimity, gentleness and humility that their success in diplomacy was great; such powers of discernment that they were sought out as spiritual counselors; and such expertise in the one-to-one relation with God that they laid the foundations for private prayer for all the years to come. Later elaborations in spiritual theology, such as the distinction between meditation and contemplation or the degrees of perfection, all grow out of the reclusive hermit's basic experience of human alone with God.

## The Monk

What was it like, then, to be a monk? A suppliant knocking outside monastery walls would hear a gatekeeper, chosen for his age and wisdom, answer "Thanks be to God" and ask what he wanted. Any stranger but this one would be welcomed as Christ, hospitably greeted, fed and housed, but the suppliant had to endure several days of harsh treatment or being ignored before being admitted to a guest room. After a few days of probation there, he was permitted to move into the novitiate where he spent a year under the guidance of a senior monk.

Such was the way of entrance as reflected in Benedict's Rule; and such, with modification, is still the way for novices and long-term visitors, even in such a modern, modernized, Protestant-founded, and ecumenically-aimed community as Taizé in France. When I arrived, totally unknown and with family, and announced that we would like to stay a year, an imperturbable brother beamed, batted not a lash, and proceeded to send us on wilder and wilder goose chases: to a mountaintop summerhouse that had no heating, to a nearby village barn that had no floors, and to a house that was going to but didn't quite yet exist.[8] When we had proven we were not, in any case, going away (by finding on our own and at some distance an ugly box for rent), the community opened its arms and took us in splendidly, offering us a wonderful house, with fireplace and grand piano, opposite a goat pasture and a few doors down from the little Romanesque church, where we happily spent a full liturgical year.

The Benedictine suppliant, once admitted, was warned by the novice master of the "difficulties and austerities ahead of him on the pathway to God,"[9] and was read the Rule of Benedict at the end of two months, eight months, and twelve months. At the end of the probationary period, any property was given away to the poor or to the monastery, the tonsure (ceremonial shaving, sometimes in the form of a cross) was received as a sign of this renunciation, and a vow "to be stable, obedient, and live as a monk" taken (i.e. to remain in that monastery the rest of his life and to observe hospitality, chastity, and other parts of the Rule).

A new member was received into the community as the lowest in its hierarchy (brothers received the kiss of peace, approached Communion, intoned the psalm, and took their place in the oratory according to the date and hour they had been admitted), and pledged to honor his seniors, obeying them with care, cheerfully and without hesitation or protest. If corrected by a superior, "no matter for what, he shall prostrate himself and offer satisfaction until he receives a blessing; likewise if he realizes he has angered or disturbed a superior in any way, he should do the same. Anyone who refuses to do this shall be whipped, and if he remains unreformed, let him be expelled from the monastery." Thus were conflicts eliminated and peace maintained.

This hierarchical severity was modified by the familial character of the monastery, a society of equally bound brothers under the guidance of the fatherly abbot who was elected for life. Although juniors called their seniors "Father," they were in turn addressed not as "Son" but as "Brother," and the abbot was charged with correcting and guiding his monks in such fashion as never to drive them to resentment.

The monastic group functioned physically much like a family, everything owned in common, meals and prayer taken together. Small one-story stone buildings served as dormitory for sleeping, refectory for eating, and oratory for praying — the farm sheds, kitchen, novitiate, and guest house farther away. The rooms were not large; in the early days 15 was the usual number of monks. There they lived, in fact, much like the large peasant families in the land surrounding, working the land, two meals in summer, one in winter, but with greater certainty of having something to eat and less exposure to violent attack.

In contrast to ordinary families, however, the monastic group lived under a rule which committed it to the practice of hospitality and to regular communal prayer: the *Opus Dei*, or work of God, interrupting time to remind themselves of eternity. Three daily "offices" inherited from Judaism (morning, noon, and night) came in the monasteries to number eight and were called Canonical Hours. This continual, communal prayer was the monastery's principal reason for being and its primary discipline.

The monastic schedule alternated spiritual and physical work, providing healthily balanced days rotating prayer, study, manual labor, and rest. It began at 2 a.m. when the monks rose for Nocturns, or as it was later called, Matins, about an hour's chanting of psalms. Afterward, a period of reading and writing would be interrupted at daybreak by Prime and Lauds, prayer, Scripture reading, and more chanted psalms. (Jacob Needleman reports that a group of French monks fell ill when they gave up the oxygenation of chanting the psalms.) Then followed five or six hours of work, interrupted by the shorter offices of Tierce, Sext, and None, and finally, a short period of reading, then Vespers while one could still see, collation (a short reading or a talk by the abbot), and Compline, a short office for which no light was needed. With seasonal adjustments for the shortening and lengthening of days, this was the Benedictine monk's pathway to God, day in and day out for the rest of his life, the monastic context from which came the major classics of western Christian spirituality and in which they were preserved and transmitted.

## The Basic Modes: A Drastic Shift

The monastic life of penitential asceticism resembles the eremitic in many ways. Indeed, the distinction between monk and hermit is at first glance hard to make. Even the word "monastery" comes from the Greek *monos* meaning "alone, single," because monasteries until the 5th and 6th centuries (with Cassian in the East and Benedict in the West) served as testing and training grounds for those who wanted to join the hermits in the desert, to determine whether they were fit for the eremitic way or were simply deserters from the sinking ship of civilization, suffering from the delusion that solitude automatically meant peace. Benedict himself defines both with the same martial imagery: "The Anchorites (hermits) . . . have prepared themselves in the fraternal line of battle (that is, "in a monastery waging their war under a rule and an abbot . . .") for the single combat of the hermit."[10]

Their lives likewise are spent doing many of the same things. Through simplicity and austerity of life, both seek inner transformation by their vows, their prayer, silence, fasting, and other forms of mortification. Both are men of few words, and variously observe periodic retreats, fixed daily periods of total silence, or meals taken silently or with one brother reading. Anyone who has experienced the quality of silence in the stricter monasteries may be tempted to conclude that there is no essential difference between the life of a hermit and the life of a monk.

Nevertheless, a drastic shift in the religious life occurs in the move from a solitary to a communal setting. The lives of the hermit and the monk, so seemingly similar, are in many respects opposite. The eremitical life, focusing on inner discipline, is noted for its outward freedom, variety, and extreme intensity, while the monastic group, controlling exterior circumstances, tends to foster obedience, conformity, and moderation.

Whereas the hermit was the only ultimate authority for his experience, remaining very much an autonomous individual even though he might turn to one more experienced as guide and advisor, the monk on principle accepts the authority of the abbot as God's representative on earth. The hermit's asceticism thus serves to strengthen his will for the struggle against bodily and spiritual sins, while the monk abandons self-will to that of the community, losing thereby a certain amount of autonomy and responsibility, but correspondingly gaining the assurance that he cannot be acting out of self-centeredness (and is thus doing God's will, not his own), as well as obtaining a salutary experience of ongoing relationship to others, an advantage in the task of understanding divine "otherness."

Also, all appearances to the contrary, the monk as compared to the hermit is profoundly language-centered. The core of monastic life is the prayed word of God, written, spoken, and read, as well as chanted, intoned, and heard, and past, present, and future monastic communities were solidly unified and linked to each other through obedience to the language of the common Rule, a set text governing the life of the community no matter who the abbot, even setting limits to the abbot's powers. (The Rule could be appealed to and was, as when accretions to the liturgy and dilutions of the discipline were swept away in the Cistercian reform.) A world of difference is hidden in Benedict's words "under a rule and an abbot."

Communal spiritual life thus incorporated much of the hermit's solitary way but differed from it significantly. Even the silence of the monastery could perhaps be said to be un-eremitical, more a controlling of language than a true silence. The hierarchical, familial structure to which the monk had to conform, with its reliance on a common verbal canon for cohesion and communion, radically alters that monastic "prayer, penance, and separation" which seem so eremitical. In structure, atmosphere, and external rather than internal discipline, the monastery was a radically different form, a different way of encounter with God.

These then are two basic forms of spirituality which have informed our Western spiritual tradition, both essentially celibate: the eremitical based on silence, solitude, and self, and the monastic based on the word, community, and obedience. Yet how could it be that our spirituality, all the way up through the 19th century and even for the most part today, is a celibate one? Celibates and monastics, after all, have always been in the minority, and at times made up only a tiny percentage of the population. And the range of spiritual practice within the Christian community today is enormous. The *Westminster Dictionary of Christian Spirituality* lists African spirituality with its strong sense of celebration, Baptist spirituality requiring personal response, the Cistercian way of separation from the world, and so on down the alphabet: desert spirituality, ecumenical, Franciscan, German, Hesychist, Ignatian, Johannine, Kabbalistic, Lutheran, Methodist, Neoplatonic, Orthodox, Puritan, Quaker, Russian, Scottish, Thomist, the spirituality of Vatican II, the Welsh. Only the later and rarely-used letters — U, X, Y, and Z — fail to present any well-known Christian type. It is hard to imagine that the experience of the couple could somehow be unreflected within all this variety, and people find it even harder to believe that they themselves, like Christians in the distant past, are in fact looking at their spiritual lives through the lens of celibacy and monasticism. How can this be when we live in a society where virginity and celibacy are relatively rare, where vowed celibacy is virtually nonexistent in Protestant groups, and where its necessary link with the priesthood and the holy is being questioned even in Roman Catholic circles?

Yet when we reflect on the bits of systematic theology that we know, we begin to realize that if asked to name typical Christian virtues, we can all answer "faith, hope, and charity"; if asked to name typical monastic virtues, many of us can call to mind that other triad, "poverty, chastity, and obedience"; but which of us has ever heard of a conjugal virtue? Though lists can in fact be found, who can automatically recite one? How many of us can even imagine what a conjugal virtue might be? The idea is so foreign that even seminary professors to whom I put the question have been stumped. In fact, on reflection, all our religious institutions, Protestant as well as Catholic, reflect one or other of the "celibate" ways, favoring the eremitical one-to-one-with-God practices of the hermit or the monastic community-dedicated-to-God of the monk, the conjugal partaking of but equally foreign to them both.

Just as all subsequent developments in the "religious" orders can be seen as modifications of the eremitic and monastic forms, all contemporary Christian churches can be categorized as primarily monastic or primarily eremitic in flavor, with salvation a communal affair best attained by gathering in groups unified by a common vocabulary and practice or an individual affair pursued by spontaneously following the lead of the spirit wherever and in whatever way it may be found.

This is perhaps most obvious in the liturgical churches, clearly descendants of familial and hierarchical monasticism, their architecture modeled on monastic churches, their people a community rather than an audience, their church a home from baptism to burial, their year a balanced and orderly alternation of feast and fast. Spiritual authority, as with the monks, is hierarchical, the power of blessing and of celebrating the Eucharist residing with the pastor, who in turn owes obedience to a bishop. These churches are above all deeply word-oriented, profoundly shaped and unified by set forms of prayer and yearly repetition of Scriptural readings. Spiritual discipline, like that of the monastic life, lies in the regulation of exteriors, leaving space for a wide individual inner variety.

Churches within the charismatic, evangelical or Puritan traditions echo the celibate tradition on its eremitical side, stressing congregational autonomy, individual effort and extemporaneous prayer, the inner light over external authority, and direct, personal awareness of the Holy Spirit. The intensity and sometimes anguished self-examination in their diaries and the seriousness of their self-discipline is clearly reminiscent of the lives of the desert Fathers. Early rising and hard work are valued and the struggle for victory over sin is a frequent theme. Some have set themselves apart from society by abstaining from certain activities altogether or on Sundays, from smoking, alcohol, or make-up, for example. Early Puritan itinerant preachers, Methodist circuit riders of the American frontier, tent meetings and campus crusades all testify to the pre-eminence of the temporary and the personal over the settled and communal in the history of salvation.

Just as all the churches hark back to the hermitage and the monastery, the spiritual practices taught within churches today bear the stamp of their celibate origin, some advising individuals to read their Bibles, worship or pray alone, aloud or silently, with or without words, fast and strengthen themselves through self-discipline, and serve their neighbors, much in the same way that hermits did and do; others advocating the basically monastic practices of communal strengthening through Christian fellowship and service, sharing time and resources in order to offer hospitality, to work together for social justice, to teach, comfort, and evangelize.

There are no great theological treatises on the couple, and there have been until very recently no spiritual works written from the conjugal perspective, no descriptions of the spiritual dimensions and stages of ongoing relationship. With the exception of material emanating from the Marriage Encounter movement and a small handful of theologians and other writers, works across the theological spectrum continue to focus exclusively on eremitical and monastic themes. The Roman Catholic William Johnston writes of stillness and silence,[11] the popular French Protestant Jacques Ellul of prayer as combat,[12] Episcopalians Alan Jones and Margaret Miles of the desert way,[13] Southern Baptist E. Glenn Hinson about the contemplative life,[14] and nondenominational Elizabeth O'Connor from the socially-involved Church of the Saviour in Washington, D.C. on the necessity of retreat.[15]

Theologians throughout the years have remarked on this lack of sustenance for couples. The Anglican U. T. Holmes wrote that marriage as a path to Christ remains "a yet undeveloped theme of spirituality,"[16] and the Roman Catholic Donald Goergan, that "our theology of sexuality must be thought through in the light of an eschatological perspective."[17] Paul Evdokimov from the Eastern Orthodox tradition lamented that successful love has neither history nor literature, and that there is no archetype of the conjugal being.[18] The spiritual literature which was available until the last few years could aptly be summarized by the title of an article by Charles Olson who is, I believe, Presbyterian: "The Closet (private), the House (familial), and the Sanctuary (communal)."[19] Even Ernest Boyer, who fully realized the lack of fit between traditional spirituality and his own life, treated marriage only cursorily and ended up elaborating a familial piety hardly distinguishable from the Benedictine monastic pattern adopted in the Renaissance by Thomas More.[20]

## Historical Transmission

The reasons for this neglect of the couple are historical and easily stated, beginning with the Bible. Celibacy has been an honorable Christian option from the beginning. Although in Jewish scripture, and at the time of Jesus, marriage had been the expected "religious" state, a duty "according to the law of Moses and the Jews" (one rabbi went so far as to say that a man who does not marry is not fully a man!),[21] from the earliest Christian times spiritual fruitfulness was recognized alongside the physical and the barren were no longer put to shame. Within Christian scripture itself, widows were taking vows of celibacy to serve the church (I Tm. 5:9-12), and by 110 A.D. celibate vows had become comparable to marriage vows and required the bishop's consent. By the 3rd century (though the practice doubtless existed long before), there is evidence for a lifelong vow of celibacy, and by the fourth, a full liturgical celebration of it "in the face of the church."[22] There thus came to be within the early Christian church two parallel ways of commitment in life: the commitment to live in conjunction with another human being, and the celibate commitment to live alone or as part of an intentional community.

Although these two ways should logically have complemented each other and each produced its own spiritual literature, fate decreed that the cities which were the earliest centers of Christian activity should be abandoned and fall into ruin after the fall of the Roman Empire. It was therefore largely in monasteries isolated from society that the Scriptures and Christian records were preserved down through medieval times, with the result that only the celibate side of spirituality was encouraged, recorded, and transmitted. Spiritual practice developed in a celibate context. It was therefore designed and most appropriate for those whose lives on principle excluded on-going sexual activity.

Thus, throughout most of Christian history only the amount of sexual activity necessary for carrying on the human race was sanctioned by the church. In the 2nd century, Clement of Alexandria allowed unenjoyed and procreative sex only during 12 hours out of the 24 (at night),[23] but by the Middle Ages, preposterous as it now seems, the Church forbade it 40 days before the important festival of Christmas, 40 days before and eight days after the more important festival of Easter, eight days after Pentecost, the eves of feastdays, on Sundays in honor of the resurrection, on Wednesdays to call to mind the beginning of Lent, Fridays in memory of the crucifixion, during pregnancy and 30 days after birth (40 if the child is female), during menstruation, and five days before communion![24]

This all adds up to 252 excluded days, not counting feastdays. If there were 30 of those (a guess which may, in fact, be on the conservative side), there would then have been 83 remaining days in the year when (provided, of course, that the woman did not happen to be menstruating or pregnant or in the post-natal period, and provided that they intended procreation) couples could with the permission of the Church have indulged in (but not enjoyed) sexual intercourse! Thus were married people continually nudged toward celibacy.

From early times the sexual life was considered at best irrelevant to spirituality and, at worst, an impediment to it. Basil in the 4th century wrote that the monastic was the ideal Christian life,[25] and that marriage was "opposed to preoccupation with the concerns of God," although he admitted that it was "allowed and blessed."[26] Jerome (340-420), on the other hand, virulently attacked it, finding it all but incompatible with prayer; and by the end of the 4th century, the superiority of celibacy was taken for granted.

Down through the ages, therefore, those who tried to help non-celibates develop spiritual "rules of life" (the Roman Catholic François de Sales in France, as well as the Protestant Lancelot Andrewes in England) could only propose "celibate" programs which led lay people farther and farther from their conjugal and worldly vocations. Spiritual directors piled prayer upon celibate prayer until none could keep up with the regimen, and finally settled for a minimal "do what you can," a diluted version of the "full" celibate way.

The first spiritual manuals written specifically for couples, from the 8th or 9th century, clearly illustrate this celibate bias. These in effect counsel *boni coniugati*, or "good spouses," to imitate monks insofar as they can: to wear simple clothes, pray privately, and lead an austere life under the direction of a bishop or an abbot. In 844, for example, a certain Jonas of Orleans recommends practices obviously drawn from the Benedictine monastic rule, including prayer and confession each day, Scripture reading, frequent prayer in church, and of course abstinence or quite severely restricted sex.

Before the end of the medieval period, the incorporation of the laity into the monastic pattern was formally accomplished in the establishment of "third orders" for the married (male monastics constituted the first order, their female counterparts the second), an institution which survives down to today. It is no surprise that questions about the "religious couple" until recently brought forth only mention of Little Gidding and Herrnhut, third orders and intentional communities, and that fervent couples of Roman Catholic or Eastern Orthodox backgrounds sometimes separated to enter monastic communities.

Protestants, of course, long ago did away with vowed celibates, or at least demoted them from the position of superiority which they had occupied since the 4th and 5th centuries, when Vigilantius of Comminges, who asserted that celibacy was heresy and the desert, desertion, was himself declared a heretic. Yet the influence of celibacy extends in subtle and unrealized ways into the Protestant tradition as well as the Roman Catholic. When the Reformation occurred in the 16th century, it did bring about change, "transferring the school of sanctity from the cloister to the family," but for sexual attitudes and spiritual practice, the transformation was not as great as one would at first suppose.

Though Protestant theologians no longer held sexual love to be heretical, and its clergy were no longer forbidden to marry, and though marriage was again proclaimed superior to celibacy by Thomas Becon,[27] among others, Luther in fact still considered sex unclean[28]; and for Calvin, though sex itself was holy and honorable, sexual pleasure (because it was "immoderate") was somehow still evil.[29] The ancient Sarum rite on which the 1549 Anglican Prayer Book was based recognized *henosis,* the joining as one-flesh, to be the essential purpose of marriage, bringing about a unique kind of unity, built by perseverance through grace; but in 1786 the words "with my body I thee worship," which had been present in the nuptial rite at least since 1125,[30] were removed from the marriage vows. And while 17th century Puritans wrote that "merry-age" was "a sweet compound of spiritual affection and carnal attraction," and taught that sensuous love should "continue unabated, with full intensity of youthful desire, throughout the whole of married life,"[31] the only part of Puritan sexual teaching which has persisted in the popular mind and language is that pleasure is evil. H. L. Mencken is said to have defined Puritanism as "the haunting fear that someone, somewhere, might be happy"!

Ancient reservations about marriage were transmitted with surprisingly little change all the way down to modern times. The Roman Catholic Church (aside from a brief excursus in the counter-Reformation) has only recently become more hospitable to the conjugal. Though Vatican II began a process of renewal and change, celibacy is still required for its clergy, who are still formed daily by the Breviary, a version of the monastic offices required for the secular clergy since the 6th century. Celibacy is still enshrined in the language, "religious" almost invariably meaning someone in an order rather than "godly," and as late as the mid-20th century Pope Pius XII was still holding that in marriage "(there is) in God's eyes, something which is held back, not completely given."[32] We can see this same false dualism similarly at work, but in reverse, in one modern Anglican's difficulties with marriage. Sheldon Vanauken's autobiographical account reveals that he thinks his wife's commitment to

Christ necessitates a lesser commitment to their marriage; that is, he thinks, like Pius XII, that God and the spouse are in competition.

Even more so have negative attitudes toward sex persisted through the ages. Most churches have begun reevaluating sexual issues in the light of incarnational theology. The United Church of Christ, for example, issued a ground breaking study of human sexuality in 1977. But letters to the editor suggest that a great number of rank-and-file Christians still assimilate sex to "the world, the flesh, and the devil," and the society at large still tends to assume that for the church, sin and sex are nearly synonymous. Although the walls are coming down, the separation of sex and spirituality which has been operative since the 4th century has yet to be completely eliminated.

There is no better way of supporting the accuracy of this historical analysis and its persistence throughout the centuries than by observing the dominance of celibacy in the saints' lives. Collections of saints' lives, like literary anthologies, distill past tradition for the present, influencing and helping to determine who will be remembered in the future. Few of the saints whose lives are readily accessible in commonly available collections are married ones, and as scholars agree (cf. Delooz's exhaustive study of canonization[33] and Cunningham's updated, English equivalent),[34] of these few, none were canonized as models of conjugal virtue.

The conjugal relationship, as portrayed in saints' lives (a fairly flabbergasting summary of the conjugal categories represented is included as an appendix), is unenlightening at best, and in the aggregate downright comical (including a few touches of black humor). Marriage in the saints' lives, particularly in its sexual aspect, is frequently portrayed as antithetical to holiness. It is in every instance irrelevant to canonization. It is viewed for the most part as highly undesirable and, in some cases, even an instrument of mortification and martyrdom. Holy conjugality in the few instances it appears is referred to rather than described, and always minimized and molded insofar as possible to fit the celibate stereotype. The celibate ideal (including the virginal marriage of Mary) is the only one provided by the canonized saints.

The major problem confronting conjugal spirituality, however, is not a sexual but a formal one. The couple, being both singular and plural, has had no models in the past, and flounders along in the present trying to speak to God with some variant of the traditional private or communal forms, which are alien to its particularity. There are no publicly available patterns for couples feeling called as such to some intensity in Christ, for developing the Christian couple as couple, and very few prayers which grow out of and reflect the peculiarity of being more than one and only two. Even the one rite which exists, the wedding ceremony, has historically been appropriated by celibate orders for an initiatory rite, and "spiritual marriage" in the tradition refers not to conjugality but to the mystics' solitary ecstasy. Couples have as yet had little choice but to look at the spiritual life with monastic eyes.

For despite the fact that Reformation priests and monks and theologians began to take wives, and in spite of the theoretical elevation of marriage, no prayer forms emerged which reflected the radically different conjugal state. Spirituality was only transferred from inside to outside the walls, not reformed from celibate to conjugal. The new wine of conjugality was poured at the Reformation into old bottles of inherited form, and in a reversal of the proverbial saying, the old bottles held, and the new wine was spoiled. Individuals continued in a one-to-one relation with God using traditional private devotions; and families, being structurally similar to the monastic community, adapted monastic piety.

The *Primer for Laity* of 1539, for example, was simply an English version of the monastic *Opus Dei*[35]; and the Anglican church eventually condensed the seven daily monastic offices into two, which were eventually further abbreviated and proposed for family prayer at home. The model for private Anglican piety was a collection of lengthy, formal, verbal prayers by Bishop Lancelot Andrewes: Biblically-based, and often quite moving, but obviously for individual, not conjugal, use. Just as Bunyan's Protestant pilgrim sets out without his wife, Thomas More's English household, well-known through the film *A Man for All Seasons*, was still in essence a "little order," as the Dominican theologian Peregrin had already spoken of the family in 1300,[36] its abbot now the father. Roland Bainton describes the typical Reformation household as a place "where the father was priest as well as magistrate, where family prayers and recital of catechism were daily exercises."[37]

Because celibate spirituality, individual and familial, was so nearly sufficient, so seemingly comprehensive, couples after the Reformation continued on with private and communal forms ill-adapted to their more-than-verbal and forcibly informal relationship, their differently-organized, differently-unified, differently-reconciled state of being. Spirituality, public and private, retained a monastic or eremitic, "one-alone-with-God" character even where marriage and celibacy were theoretically equal vocations. Because no conjugal forms were available, lay people continued to measure themselves against the existing celibate models, falling always short of "perfection." As the Methodist theologian John Kent (somewhat uncharitably!) put it, "There is something more than slightly comic in the spectacle of young married ministers who have no intention of putting away their wives haunting the courts of Taizé as a way, one supposes, of sublimating their sense of guilt at not being more completely devoted to God."[38]

## Couples Need a Conjugal Spirituality

The fact that spirituality as we know it is basically celibate is not a new idea, but one whose implications have not been grasped by spiritual counsellors and writers. None yet, as Evdokimov suggested, teach the Upanishads and Tantric writings as the basis of moral theology for couples.[39] Some still refuse to grant that mystical experience can be associated with erotic love. Gerald May, for example, accepts as "true unitive experience" only that in which awareness is "clear and *wide open*, excluding nothing,"[40] and Elizabeth Achtemeier denies that knowledge of God is communicated in sex.[41] Others still advocate dealing with "spiritual" experience in isolation from life circumstances. For a married woman of 40 who "finds herself more and more irritable with her husband and children," and God far away, Barry and Connelly prescribe that she "be helped to voice her desire for a closer relationship to the God who can respond to that desire."[42]

Even those who recognize that the spirituality which we have inherited is celibate often do not realize just how insufficient that spirituality is for couples in a modern environment. It is clear that marriage before the 20th century was often only an economic or political arrangement to channel the disruptive forces of sexuality, to provide for the education of children, and to insure the orderly transmission of property. It was easily assimilable to the familial structure whose spiritual needs could be supplied by the monastic model. But today couples exist before children, do not cease to exist even with children, often continue to exist after children have left the nest or even died, and some, deliberately or involuntarily, exist without ever having children at all. Couples are no longer, if they ever were, a subsidiary, transitional phenomenon on the way toward a familial group.

In addition, relationships are becoming more and more egalitarian (a recent newspaper article reported that bishops were counselling Roman Catholic husbands to share the housework!), and even where couples have chosen to adopt a hierarchical structure, intensity and amplitude of relationship modify the old model. The unit "two-in-full-relation" (I've been told of a certain priest who once with a slip of the tongue joined a couple "in woe-ly headlock"!) is radically different from either the "two one's" of the eremitic tradition or the "two-in-a-group" of monasticism. The prayers of the one and the many simply no longer (if they ever did) suffice.

I first came to suspect this through reflecting on my own experience and that of friends with whom I talked. My suspicion was strengthened by talks with retreat directors puzzling over the problems of spiritual direction for married people. One of the few monks who concern themselves with such matters, Pierre-Yves Emery of Taizé, noted the difficulty that couples have in sustaining a joint prayer life, and speculated that it was because of the lack of common religious background (though this reason seemed counter to the common wisdom at that ecumenical brotherhood that it is prayer which creates unity, not the other way around). The retreat director and author Ron Delbene remarked during a workshop on spiritual development in the parish that traditional practice results frequently in the dissolution of couples, especially when undertaken by only one of the pair. This could well be the end result in the example of the married woman given in Barry and Connelly's book on spiritual direction.

As a concrete historical example illustrating the inadequacy of traditional prayer for couples, I would like to cite the case of Martin Luther, a pivotal figure, first monk, then married. Luther (1483-1546) was an Augustinian friar and a professor of theology deeply concerned with the spiritual life in theory and in practice. He left his community in Wittenberg and eventually married an ex-nun. What better teachers of conjugal prayer, one would think, than two specialists in the spiritual life who marry. Yet, though Luther considered marriage, like the monastery, "a school for sanctity," he and his wife apparently failed to find in conjugal prayer the same satisfaction they had experienced in the monastery. According to Anne Fremantle, he declared that he and his wife "did not pray as fervently after as they used to before their marriage."[43] Though Luther and his wife seem to have interpreted this experience as personal lack and failure, I suggest that they were in fact experiencing what all new couples before and since have experienced: that their old way of prayer no longer expressed the whole of their lives, that the familiar and well-loved forms of traditional spirituality were inadequate for their expanded being as coupled individuals.

Although it will require a drastic shift in outlook, a shift as radical as the one from solitude to community, the time has come to focus on the conjugal and sexual dimensions of the spiritual life, to recognize the couple as a theologically significant unit, and to develop a spirituality which can reflect the couple's paradoxical nature and distinctive lifestyle. Fortunately, though spiritual counselling is still by and large unavailable, a growing number of religiously-minded couples have begun to speak out about experiencing God within a context of their physical and emotional intimacy, and a number of important works have appeared. The work of constructing a systematics for conjugal spirituality can now begin.

# 2

# Conjugal Spirituality

---

A CONJUGAL SPIRITUALITY is one which takes seriously the fact that humans can exist only in more or less intimate relation to that which is outside of themselves, and that they are always acting to a greater or lesser degree in conjunction with realities other than their own. This is a radical departure from the traditional spirituality which sees discrete individuals as the locus of spiritual value and the couple as two individuals on separate journeys to spiritual growth, from that of Scott Peck, for example, who writes that "the genuine lover always perceives the beloved as someone who has a *totally* (my emphasis) separate identity."[1]

Conjugal spirituality points to the possibility of a shift of the center of spiritual attention from within individuals to the spaces between them, to their encounters and to the interpenetration which sometimes results. It is a spirituality which looks for the presence and action of God in relationships and in their impact, and which affirms the couple as a spiritually and theologically significant unit. Broadly speaking, a conjugal spirituality is relevant to everyone, since "no one is an island." Most narrowly and specifically, it concerns itself with the fullest example and archetype of relation, long-term, intimate coupledom, and with its discipline of radical proximity.

The dyadic way in its fullest development is an adventure in newness, in paradoxically impossible two-in-oneness. The person who enters upon long-term intimate coupledom experiences an otherward shift of center within the self, the creation of a joint reality in the space between the self and other, and a degree of interpenetration significant enough to effect the whole of their being, including the spiritual life. The prayer of a partnered person is not the same as the prayer of the unpartnered.

I have chosen "conjugal" to designate this practice of proximity because its root words, *con-* and *jugium* mean "yoked together," an appropriate verbal parallel to the names of the familiar spiritual types, the "eremitic" (the adjectival form of "hermit," from Greek words meaning "desert" and "solitary") and the monastic or "cenobitic" (meaning "having meals in common" i.e. living in community).

"Conjugal" is a better word than "sexual" for this new form of spirituality because although sexual activity distinguishes the celibate from the noncelibate in the popular mind, and although the *Westminster Dictionary of Spirituality* recognizes the existence of sexuality as a "recent development in the history of Christian spirituality,"[2] it is quite possible for "sexual" spiritualities to be centered on practice which is profoundly "celibate" in nature. The disciplines of tantrism, for example, do not necessarily involve another human being, or when they do, at least in some schools, it is only for ritual or symbolic purposes.

The word "conjugal" is also more appropriate than the term "marital," even when conjugal is used in its narrowest application to refer to the long-term couple. Marriage and its related words, as etymology demonstrates, are ultimately linked to social rather than personal ends. "Marital" has its root in the Latin word "mater" meaning mother, which tells us that marriage as an institution was in its origins a structure designed to protect women made vulnerable through child-bearing, and thus to strengthen society's ability to perpetuate itself. The word "marital" is an institutional rather than a relational term, referring not to the union of two people but to a social status or construct.

Conjugal, however, "yoked together," can side-step both of these difficulties. Despite the fact that dictionaries and common usage make it synonymous with "marital" and "matrimonial," its origins tell us that it points more directly and unequivocally to connection itself, to the community of being which constitutes a couple rather than to the community of purpose which founds a family. The Latin verb *con-jungere* means "to bind together, connect, or join (as in the Indian spiritual discipline of *yoga*), unite (especially by ties of relationship or friendship)," and "to put on an equality with." The word "conjugal" implies cooperation, reciprocity, and mutuality.

Conjugal spirituality today is what one would have to categorize as a "popular spirituality," a system which can be reconstructed only by putting together bits and pieces, as in a mosaic. Found more in practice than in language, more in ritual than in dogma, in sacramentals rather than in sacraments, its historical documents, as with other popular spiritualities, have survived primarily in the attacks of its critics, in sermons, in inscriptions, in art and archeology, and in secular literature. We learn where to look by reading about heresies, just as one can find the "juicy" parts of the Bible by noting what Bernard forbade (the beginnings of Genesis and Ezekiel, and all of the Song of Songs!) to those of his brothers under 30, the age at which their priestly ministry began. We find it in Chaucer, Donne, and *Jitterbug Perfume* rather than *The Imitation of Christ* or *The Ladder of Perfection.*

It is perhaps only in our day that a fully developed conjugal spirituality—a spirituality which recognizes that whenever relationship occurs, something radically new comes into being—has become a real possibility. To speak of radical proximity as spiritual journey is to explore as yet uncharted territory. Yet great though the change may be when we finally accomplish it, an evolutionary leap in the history of spirituality, it is nevertheless not a total break with the past.

## Historical Traces

From this point in time, when we look back through history we have access to documents which have long been lost to us, and we are thus able to identify the existence of the conjugal path despite the bias of the written record. The mainstream developments which were described in Chapter 1 are by no means the whole story. Though few and discontinuous, there are traces of a different way, suggesting the *de facto* existence of a parallel, underground tradition which either survived despite official neglect or was reinvented by succeeding generations of couples.

Aside from the more substantial sources which will be mentioned in later chapters, many fragments from early times onward suggest that a conjugal worldview has always existed within the Christian community. Synesius of Cyrene, in 155 A.D., resisted attempts to force him to give up his wife before becoming bishop, saying that such separation would be "impiety," and John of Chrysostom (335-407) wrote that the couple when truly united was an image of God. Even after the celibate lifestyle became the sole spiritual model in the 4th century, we hear echoes and distant reverberations of the conjugal, sometimes with traceable influence from one to the other, sometimes not. We know a little, for example, of Maximus the Confessor (580-662). He taught that the love of God and of humans were not two different things, but two aspects of a single total love, and that Christ unified the sexes in his own nature, in the Resurrection being "neither man nor woman, though he was born and died a man."[3]

We know that Maximus influenced John Scot Erigena. John taught that Christ anticipated a final reintegration which would begin on the human level and continue up through all planes of being to the divine.[4] We know that Aelred of Rievaulx (1110-1167) wrote that sex could be a means to contemplation, and that Christ is present between two lovers as the Holy Spirit to the Father and the Son.[5] We know that Alain de Lille (1128-1202) recognized the part sex played in creating the community of life. Scholars have also preserved at least the names of other theologians who recognized the conjugal way in some fashion — the Englishman Richard Middleton (1271), Martin LeMaistre, Thomas Sanchez, a Jesuit of the 15th century, the Scotsman John Major in the 16th century, Erasmus, Vives, Todd. Doubtless many more remain to be discovered, like Scupoli (1530-1610), who taught that conjugal asceticism included the duty of maximizing physical pleasure.

It is in the Jewish and the Eastern Orthodox traditions, however, that the conjugal way was present with anything like depth and continuity. Although the Eastern Orthodox tradition was even more strongly marked by celibate monasticism than the Western Church, and although Jewish thinking on marriage and sexuality was thoroughly patriarchal and interpreted in a human context which valued procreation over relationship, from these two religious cultures came the impetus and much of the matter for the developments in conjugal spirituality which are taking place today.

In the 19th century, many Russian writers fled to France and Eastern Orthodox theology became more accessible in the West. First came the news that a Russian Archimandrite, Alexander J. Bukharev, had caused a sensation in his community when he requested and received reduction from priest to lay status and subsequently married, thereby putting into question the superiority of the celibate way of life over the conjugal.[6] Later in the century, a theologian who settled in Paris, Vladimir Soloviev, combining the insights of orthodoxy with ancient Jewish conjugal traditions as they had evolved in 13th-century Kabbalistic teachings, taught that love, and chiefly sexual love, was the necessary and irreplaceable basis for all spiritual progress.[7] Marriage was in his view superior to celibacy as a path to sanctity; in Soloviev, the pendulum had swung to the opposite extreme.

The Jews, under an obligation to "go forth and multiply," never developed an institutionalized celibacy. Their highest religious leader is even obliged to be married[8]; and Hebrew scripture guarantees women the three fundamental unqualified rights of food, clothing, and the *onah* (sexual intercourse apart from the duty to procreate). The commandment of *onah* includes not mere physical performance, but also closeness and joy, involving the total personality. It was a Jewish theologian, Martin Buber, who was finally the first to proclaim: "In the beginning is the relation,"[9] a theme since taken up by others, including theologians such as Carter Heyward and Sam Keen. For Buber all spiritual reality is essentially conjugal; our primary spiritual contact takes place not within but around us.

## Modern Development — Secular and Religious

The real beginning of conjugal spirituality, however, is usually placed in the 20th century, in the period between the two World Wars. It was particularly noticeable in France, where groups of couples began to form, to meet, and to share their experiences (much of which is documented in Henri Caffarel's journal, *Anneau d'or*); but Spain also saw the development of weekend retreats, which were to blossom into an international Marriage Encounter movement exploring couples and spirituality.[10]

While there are many works from the 40s and 50s which could be mentioned, it was from the 60s onward that works of conjugal spirituality began to appear in any numbers. In 1962 the first substantial work of what one could properly call conjugal spirituality appeared, Evdokimov's *Sacrament of Love.*[11] Clergy couples were becoming visible presences within various denominations, and couples began increasingly to reflect and write jointly on the spiritual dimensions of their experience, as evidenced by the books of Joseph and Lois Bird, who write as counsellors,[12] Evelyn and James Whitehead, a psychologist/theologian team, and the many evangelical sex and marriage manuals. Publications came thick and fast: Biblical and historical studies,[13] works focused on pastoral issues,[14] works from secular disciplines, such as psychology[15] and sociology[16] — so that it is now possible to envisage the beginnings of a systematic spiritual theology for couples, to recognize the human phenomenon of coupledom as the locus of a spiritual organism comparable to that of the soul for the individual and the spirit for the community, and to explore the joint practices conducive to its growth, the virtues and problems peculiar to its life, and its conjugal stages of ascetic and mystical progress. It is possible, in a word, to speak of a conjugal spirituality; former heresy, present possibility.

It should not go unmentioned that changing social conditions contributed substantially to this changing theological climate. Although Lawrence Stone places the beginning of companionate marriage from 1640 to 1800, more recent factors, including the changed situation of women and new attitudes toward sexuality, have profoundly altered the couple whose nature seemed so immutable. No longer, for example, do women frequently die in childbirth, as did Cranmer's first wife in the first year of their marriage. One might search in vain for a pre-20th-century theologian married for longer than 20 years. Jeremy Taylor's wife, for example, died less than 13 years after their marriage, Calvin's after nine. Anne More bore 12 children and died 16 years after her marriage to John Donne. The longevity of contemporary Western woman means that there has been a dramatic increase in the number of 50-year couples. Whereas the average marriage in 1911 was 28 years, it was 42 in 1967. For the first time in history, substantial numbers of people of all sorts and conditions have the possibility of choosing, and even some chance of getting the conjugal way, that 50-year experiment in the closest, most intense imaginable community.

The change in the status of women in the 20th century has been equally important in the evolution of the couple. The possibility of being paid for work has made contemporary women more independent as persons and more equal as partners in relationship. More than ever coupledom has become a matter of choice (which is to say, vocation) rather than semi-necessity for women. The possibility of divorce has transformed marriage from an institution to an adventure for men and women alike, while the human potential movement explored the means for honest relating.

Finally, attitudes toward things sexual have radically changed. The contraceptive choices available enhance the recreational aspects of intercourse, and greater openness and knowledge have led to the appreciation of sex as the basic pulse of human life and a means of communicating and increasing unitive love. As one Roman Catholic theologian put it: "With birth control, sex is now in a purer, more meaningful form . . . Sex is now not only a process of creation of new life but of identity . . . a means of self-expression, activating one's particular human potentialities for love and commitment."[17] As Paul Avis points out, Davis in 1976, Nelson in 1979, and Dominian in 1987 each affirm that sexual union in marriage can be sacramental of God.[18]

Twentieth-century developments in mainstream theology have also prepared the way for the emergence of conjugal spirituality. An upsurge of interest in the spiritual life and a renaissance in mystical studies have widened the domain of spirituality beyond the borders of confessional boundaries and the bounds of organized religion, leading to the recognition (by substantial contingents, Catholic and Protestant alike) of "Protestant mystics," of the communal and liturgical dimensions of mysticism, of the feminine dimensions of the divine, of Eastern traditions, both Eastern Orthodox and non-Christian, and of "secular" varieties of mystical experience, those elicited by "natural triggers" such as scenery, art, beauty, and introspection on the passive side, or active movement, childbirth, creative work, and even sex.[19] All these expansions of knowledge have contributed in one way or other to making conjugal spirituality possible.

There have been advances in theory as well. Spiritual theologians of widely different persuasions now consider that the difference between the ordinary and the mystical is one of degree rather than one of kind, and some have even begun to mention possible correlations between the traditional spiritual stages and normal human development.[21] As early as 1902, the philosopher William James pointed out research showing close parallels between the youthful phenomenon of "conversion" in evangelical circles and general adolescent development between the ages of 14 and 17 (passage into maturity after a period of introspection and depression).[22] And in the 70s the Jesuit William Johnston wrote that "it is not impossible that these trials of John of the Cross (which have been associated with the 'second conversion' in other authors) take place in many cases at a definite period in life; that is to say, in Jung's 'middle period of life,' a time of psychic toil and trouble occurring after the age of thirty-five."[23] Herbert Slade likewise writes that John's dark night "often coincides with physical periods of life such as middle age and the menopause."[24]

All of these developments in related areas, both secular and religious, have came together in our century to make a space for the couple in the spiritual scheme. In 1974 Donald Goergan, in *The Sexual Celibate*, wrote that "the dichotomy between sexuality and spirituality and between celibacy and marriage is destructive and inappropriate. Integration lies in seeing how we can be both sexual and spiritual simultaneously and in seeing that choosing one way of life does not imply the inferiority of the other."[25]

Though couples have long been almost invisibly submerged in family and society, we are finally in a position today to make use of bits and pieces which have fortuitously survived (some of which I have gathered in an appendix) to begin to construct a conjugal spirituality.

# 3

# The Human Phenomenon:
# Coupledom

IN ORDER TO MAKE CONJUGAL SPIRITUALITY PLAUSIBLE, it will first be useful to take a closer look at the largely unexamined and deceptively familiar human reality which underlies it, to remember just how peculiar and paradoxical "pairdom" and "coupledom" are.

The concept of "couple" seems a quite ordinary one, a standard, well-known social unit. Fragile though it might be, it has been and continues to be universal as a cultural choice, the principal means whereby the great majority of people find pleasure, combat loneliness, or finitude, and order the deep forces of soul and body. The process by which people enter into more or less formal agreements to share each others' lives represents the most important legal contract in every human society.

## Mystery and Paradox

Yet this ordinary social unit and inevitable human phenomenon has always posed great difficulties to society. Is it kinship, partnership, or coinherence? Secular and religious jurisdictions alike have continually struggled to set its boundaries, but they remain unclear, sometimes even to the couples themselves. What brings coupledom into legal or canonical existence, ritual or living together, consent or coitus? Which of its elements are essential to its continuance? Cohabitation? Faithfulness? Harmony? Rabbis argued such points before canonists, and secular judges today face increasingly complicated versions of the same problems. How do we know for a certainty when or that a couple has ceased to exist? Courts sometimes find that couples applying for divorce are simultaneously infringing on the conditions for obtaining one by continuing to live together as husband and wife. I know of one couple who say their divorce just isn't working out!

Boundaries have been and will continue to be hard to legislate. Coupledom is undefinable in its essence and protean in form. Although monogamy predominates in most countries, the *Encyclopedia Britannica* notes that "as a unique and exclusive form, it is very rare outside of modern Western culture."[1] Pre-Christian culture recognized at least five kinds of marriage (same sex, opposite sex, with kids, with property, and one-year), and in our society today alternative forms seem to proliferate endlessly (free love, dyadic with or without non-consensual adultery, swinging, open, intimate friendship, contractual agreement, cohabitation, monogamous or non-monogamous, hetero- or homosexual). Coupledom is unique among human relationships, hopelessly paradoxical in nature, two yet one. Law and the society have both found it expedient to resolve the paradox by declaring the couple a unit.

The law has traditionally treated it as a kind of fictitious legal entity similar to that of the corporation, and represented by the person of the husband. As late as the 18th century, the English jurist Blackstone wrote: "By marriage, the husband and wife are one person in law; that is, the very being or legal existence of the woman is suspended during the marriage, or at least is incorporated and consolidated into that of the husband . . ."[2] This principle of unity, though passed on from English to American law, is now supplemented or replaced by the principles of contract law, under which spouses are regarded not as the corporation itself but as two partners within it. "One plus one equals one" has now in law become "One plus one equals two one's." Yet this solution sidesteps rather than solves the problem. Any two people are two ones.

Societies would also like to avoid the paradox. They have tried to resolve it by considering coupledom as a kind of blood kinship.[3] Blood kinship, however, like the legal "principal of unity," is fiction, not fact, and sidesteps the question of what the couple is in itself. In addition, the concept has difficulties of its own.

Marriage is clearly less than kinship. Blood relations are ines-capable. One can reject parents or disinherit children, but their claims to relationship will never cease to exist. It is built into our language. When marriage is terminated, the partner becomes an ex-spouse, rather like an ex-friend, but one can never speak of an ex-fa-ther or ex-sister. Yet the primary marital bond is also closer than kinship. In our society, a spouse takes precedence over one's other kin, and will, for example, be given admittance to a hospital before other relatives or friends. The marriage rite is in effect a public dec-laration that both society and I will consider this human being whom I have chosen as henceforth in an even closer relation to me than those whom I did not and could not choose.

The idea which lies behind most books on conjugal prayer, that the couple is essentially a group composed of two individuals, is also partially unsatisfactory. While it is true that in a couple there are always two individuals, even a pair is not a true group, not even a small one, much less a couple. Unlike the group, a pair is structur-ally different, depending on the continued adhesion of all its mem-bers for its very existence, and the dynamics of two are different from the dynamics of even three. Eyes can look at and ears can hear only one person at a time, so that group relations are always more complex but less intense than the relation of one to one.

If we doubt this fact, we can experience its truth for ourselves by making two short experiments. First, we can slowly and deliber-ately sweep our eyes across a given space, noticing their movement. Close observation shows us that the eyes can only focus on one point at a time and that they do not even glide smoothly from one object to the next, but instantaneously hop over whatever lies in between. Though we have the capacity for shifting focus quickly and for a partial, peripheral vision, we can fully look at only one thing at a time.

We might think nevertheless that hearing is different, that we can hear what two people are saying if we wish; but one minute of listening to a simultaneous stream of talk from both sides of the head will prove that we are simply switching attention from one ear to the other, getting perhaps most or even in some cases all of the essential content if we are adept and rapid enough, but in fact getting the sen-sory input consecutively, not simultaneously.

Thus we see with our eyes that a pair is not one and we realize upon reflection that it is not a group. Yet when thrust back on its simple twoness for definition, we land definitively in paradox for, being built essentially on community of being, not on community of purpose, the couple is not only two but more than two persons. Coupledom involves interpenetration of being, and more than the kind of interpenetration which occurs in every relationship. It involves a progressive intermingling of lives which has been interpreted by romantics such as Charles Williams as a unitive state which he calls "coinherence," and which even realists recognize as an intermingling so great that it can take on the density of a third, personal reality, a "We." One couple has called it a "third self" and given it a name formed by joining letters of their own personal names.[4]

The couple, in sum, is both one and not one, two and not two, more than "two one's" in intensity and scope, less than a group in structure, and different from either in its way of relating. Though it is a unit, it can never be simply "one," as social and legal institutions would find most convenient, and although it is "two persons," to extract the individuals entirely from the third reality that is their dyadic context is to falsify their being. Before so total and complex an association institutions stand perplexed. The questions raised are as mysterious as those of life itself, and no universally acknowledged answers are available. In the last analysis the couple remains a paradox, a mystery even to itself, trying to achieve the impossible, to cause to be that which is not, to bring into being a more-than-blood relationship by sheer act of will. Small wonder, then, that its spirituality should so long remain undiscovered.

## Unique in Its Formation

The couple begins not with "falling in love" (since the revelation of love is the involuntary root of relationship and may happen any number of times), and not at a ceremony of commitment (which is only the public declaration and institutional acknowledgement of the couple's existence), but at that usually undeterminable moment when both are first aware of being chosen by the other. At that moment begins the first stage of conjugal life when a couple begins to create and form its being. This is a serious process which requires, some say, 9 to 14 years,[5] but which is in any case a highly complicated and lifelong task never really complete.

Just as the couple itself is unique among human relations, the way it is formed is also unique. In all other cases which an individual may face, the primary relational task is to assimilate and adapt to rules and patterns already established. A child becoming part of a school, an adult starting a new job, or a novice entering a religious community encounters a framework which is already in place. The individual can in certain cases and over time bring about changes in an institution or a family, but if one ignores the frameworks too soon or too drastically, one is likely to be excluded. Even one who enters at the top, like a new boss in the company, is wise to proceed with caution.

The formation of a couple-body is radically different from these social "incorporations" because partners in a relationship must actively collaborate in the creation of an order for which no one set pattern exists. There are two separate inner pictures, certainly, derived chiefly from the families of origin, but these pictures each have limitations. The children in whom these pictures incubated saw limited parts of the patterns which were being lived out, and understood even those parts with a child's understanding. In addition, parental patterns are sometimes of little relevance or even counterproductive to the circumstances of their children's lives and, in any case, the pictures are irreducibly two, certain to be different in many important respects.

Each couple must by trial and error discover its own unrepeatable shape. The being of a couple is not fixed but living and changing, more like a person than a piece of pottery. It will be born, grow or languish, and die. Its development follows recognizable patterns of formation and flowering, consolidation and balance. Over time, its ongoing transformations lead either to the monstrosity of deadening conflict and stalemate or the fulfillment of a durable and increasingly satisfying union. As unique as each human being, every couple is a construction without fixed pattern, arrived at by a combination of imitation, experiment, imagination and, above all, will.

The task of conjugal formation is in some ways very like the birth of a person. The couple is first "conceived" at the often unde-

finable moment when there is mutual awareness of mutual prefer-
ence, and is "born" when this mutual affinity has solidified into
something approaching certainty and commitment. In the "prenatal"
period in between, for inclination to ripen into choosing, both persons must ascertain through verbal and nonverbal interchange that
there is compatibility as well as attraction. Dialogue must establish
affinity to create a secure, supportive space where each assures to the
other a personal value. The couple becomes a unit, a community of
being, through a vision based on attraction (in spiritual terms, the
revelation, or call, that corresponds to vocation), a testing of compatibility (approximating the novitiate of a celibate vocation), and the
mutual choice which leads to explicit or *de facto* commitment. The
embryonic community takes time to take flesh and, as in all births,
something totally new comes forth. Couples are formed not by clon-
ing but by the combining of "chromosomes," by weaving imagined
and imitated strands from many old patterns into a story of their
own.

Also, like the physical growth of the individual, the process of
formation is not complete with the "birth" of commitment. In theory
some couples could embody from the beginning onward the coinherence they have glimpsed, but evidence suggests that this is rare. As
Lederer and Jackson note about marriage, for example, in one of the
most realistic of the many books on the subject: "We have never
observed a generally constant collaborative union between spouses
during the period when they are raising children."[6] Close, creative
union is the product of a combination of elements: a certain amount
of luck, a certain amount of hard work, and a sufficiency of time.

Yet there are also huge differences between the birth and
growth of an individual and that of a couple. The couple must
choose to come into existence, must cooperate in its own creation,
and bring about its own birth. Unlike the human being, it has substantial control over its own destiny from the beginning. The couple
is also obviously more complex in development. The growth of a
pair must inevitably be more varied in pattern than that of the individual, more like the intertwined snake than the rod of the caduceus.

In Gail Sheehy's assessment of male and female cycles of sexual development over a lifetime, for example, the pattern is diamond-
shaped. The partners, according to Sheehy, start out more or less

alike, then move progressively apart in capacity, availability, social roles, personality traits and overall sense of self until about age 40, at which point, according to her (dismal) theory, "they both go into a sexual involution, which eventually brings them back together in the unisex of old age"![7]

Finally, the couple is unlike the individual in that it must act for its own preservation in a much more deliberate way than the individual. Individuals might contemplate suicide, but rarely forget to eat, whereas couples often forget to nourish their relationship. The couple, having come into being through choice, can only stay in existence by consciously and unconsciously making that choice over and over again. Despite the fact that it is a natural phenomenon and a universal tendency, the couple always remains an unstable artifice, never having the solidity of real kinship, a fragile miracle dependent on the partners' continued willingness to be in relation.

## Stage One
## Creation of the Couple Shape: Con-sensus

The task of the first stage is to bring about the union of two separate beings through trial and error. By experimentation a comfortable distance between the two must be achieved, as well as agreement on their mode of communication and the degree to which they will be open and available to "outsiders." The couple tests out possibilities until it arrives at a consensus on the basics. Boundaries are gradually defined, the outline gradually takes shape, and being which has never before existed appears.

From the sociological point of view, this creation of the couple, like the Biblical creation of the world, takes place primarily through a word which is action. Emile Durkheim, the "father of sociology," spoke of couple-building as a dramatic act in which two strangers, individuals whose pasts are inevitably separate, come together and match differing definitions of reality. More recently and with greater specificity, Peter Berger and Hansfried Kellner point out that we choose as associates (particularly for long-term relationships of total intimacy, in which partners must touch at all levels) those

who share our interests, who "speak the same language."[8]  But since
no two "languages" are totally alike, a new couple must jointly establish the "vocabulary," the behavioral and bodily dialect in which they
will communicate, through a lengthy process of agreeing together
what each "word" will mean.

This building of con-sensus (literally, "sensing with") is potentially world-doubling, eyes becoming four, ears hearing from twice
as many directions, smell, taste, and touch magnified twofold. Moreover, the couple is not only constructing a new present reality for
themselves, but even reconstructing the past, as their lives before
meeting are reflected back to them from the eyes of the other. The
world as it appears to each will be slowly compared to the world as
it appears to the other. Every aspect of reality will eventually be
re-viewed and reevaluated: family, friends, possessions, Christmas
customs, past events and patterns of behavior, favorite ideas and activities, and priorities for spending time and money. The exceptional
character of first love is doubtless due in part to the fact that it is
often also the first encounter with this exhilarating process of "language" construction, of seeing and making new human reality.

The means available to the couple to achieve this new creation
all come under the heading of dialogue.  Conjugal asceticism is
based on communicating and relating, verbal and nonverbal.  Talk
and sex may seem the most natural things in the world, and indeed
they are, but using them to create long-lasting intimacy is not natural
or simple.  The couple must develop skills in active listening (para-
phrasing what one has heard to confirm its accuracy and assure the
partner that he or she has been heard), empathizing, criticizing or
confronting when disparity or discrepancy threaten, diplomacy for
conflict resolution, and above all skills in bodily relating, mastery of
the powerful force which is popularly called sex.  Whereas people as
individuals and as groups depend most heavily on words to achieve
communion with others — chitchat or constitutions — for couples
the sexual dimension is paramount, a distinguishing factor which sets
off their relating from all other ways.

This building of the couple is a lifelong work whose possibilities are great but whose difficulties should also not be minimized.
Building consensus can be difficult and even painful.  It takes creativity to make a couple which lasts, and (as Simone de Beauvoir

wryly and more truthfully than she realized has said) even a miracle. It is without doubt the most difficult thing one can ever attempt. As another French wit has so ironically put it, a durable relation may simplify your life, but it complicates your day.[9] Society and the church are pleased to preside over its beginning, but give little in the way of advice for the balancing act afterward, assuming that those whom God hath joined together live happily ever after; though modern America has shown just how unreal that happiness often is, and how quickly a couple can again become two ones when social constraints are removed.

The coming into being of something which has never before existed necessarily involves change, and change is sometimes experienced as loss. Long-term relationship in the past has usually required women to give up their names, and always entails, for both partners, the possibility of losing some degree of such things as self-sufficiency, freedom of movement and choice, old friendships and habits, personal creativity, wider social participation, and leisure!

And even when the adaptation and change involved in becoming a couple is not experienced as restriction or loss, coupledom necessarily involves abrasiveness. Inherent in the most intense form of relationship is lifelong 24-hour-a-day accountability and drastically reduced, if not totally eliminated, privacy. Penelope Washbourn writes trenchantly of the "all-pervading, ever-seeing presence of the other . . . a mirror of unmasking."[10] There is no hiding place. Every element of the personality eventually becomes manifest.

The enterprise is obviously not without reward. Each partner arrives at new self-definition since the awareness characteristic of a lover in the beloved's presence triggers new knowledge of self, new self-value and self-blame. Strengths and weaknesses, limits and abilities appear more clearly, mirrored in the other's eye. There is also new knowledge of the other, a never-ending personal knowing as masks slip and as each begins to eliminate from their picture of the other any childish projections, subconscious fantasies or social stereotypes.

The combination of relationship with physical intimacy leads to new dimensions of experience and knowledge as well. I believe it is Penelope Washbourne who has pointed out that what it is like to have sexual intercourse is the most mysterious of grown-up mysteries for the child. And beyond the initial mystery, the extraordinarily powerful uprising which tears us out of ourselves and carries us beyond our mind and senses can leave us with heightened consciousness, at peace with our partner, and naturally open to a changed world. Its long-term practice gives a full, non- and trans-rational bodily knowledge of self and other. And finally, a new world comes into being from this meeting and fitting together of two separate biographies, a world which can be a secure, supportive space where each, by selective, sympathetic perception, can help the other toward fulfillment. Charles Williams describes the transfiguration which can take place as "a mutual invasion, breaking down both selves so that both can be transformed by the love both receive."[12]

## Stage Two
## Consolidation: Equilibrium and Growth

The second stage of conjugal life can be said to begin when the couple is conscious of a past built together, a certain joint accomplishment, a creation which must thenceforward be maintained. In the second stage, as trust becomes more solid, the individuals can open themselves to each other more and more, and "the other" begins to be looked at as he or she really is, all romantic posing past. Coinherence between the two begins to grow, and this existential solidity characteristically allows the fruitfulness of the couple, thus far exercised in building up their unity, to spill over in commitment to larger values and new ventures, such as children, a joint social commitment, or separate careers.

This growth is necessary to the health of the conjugal life because present, finite selves are always exhaustible centers of interest, and if the couple wishes to continue with the same stories they have always told, they will usually be forced to search out new people to tell them to. Change and growth are necessary, but imbalance and overextension are ever-present dangers as outside commitments are taken on, as juggling is added to the balancing act. Love and loyalty are spiritual goods, able to be infinitely shared without diminishment, but concrete time, energy and attention are finite, and must be portioned out with the general assent of the other if the relationship is to remain strong. Periods of absence or intense outside commitment can put the relationship "on hold," coasting on its accumulated capital.

Therefore in addition to the beginner's disciplines, the middle-stage couple needs to cultivate the formalization of dialogue (the companionable cup of coffee in the morning, the afternoon recap over a cup of tea, or the bedtime story continued together after children can read for themselves). Structuring, balancing, and celebratory rituals must supplement verbal communication: sitting down together or having fun in whatever fashion to commemorate the coupledom that has been constructed, whatever achieves a creative equilibrium between the one, two, three, and four, between the beloved "You," the "I" of integrity, the "We" of partnership, and the "They" of outside commitment. If sacrifices are too lopsided, the self-esteem of one will suffer from the self-assertion of the other.

The couple must also cultivate that ongoing version of creativity which is called perseverance and invent new ways of growing together, for life is clinically defined as the ability to produce new cells, but also and equally importantly, the ability to assimilate them into an integrated system. Whether it be backyard ornithology or a new sailboat, pleasurable new activities within the couple's joint world must counterbalance new discoveries without. This applies to the physical as well as to the social dimension. Spontaneous at first, in the long run sex presupposes an adequate preparation in all other conjugal skills, and requires as well its own learning and discipline (mastery of self-possession and self-surrender, the ability and the will to put aside distractions, center and concentrate attention in the body, to be present and freely available to the other in awareness and trust).

There is always something new to learn about sex as liberating energy and a means to intimacy, both from personal and joint introspection as well as from outside sources: massage, for fun and to increase awareness and freedom; the contemplation of bodies as fields of double polarity (left and right, up and down) and of postures, movements, and gestures in their symbolic depth (the hands as unions of opposites, the joining of breaths as the bond of the spirit), the education of the senses as intermediaries between the high and the low, the inside and the out.[13] The ways to renewal are infinitely various. The essential is that the couple continue to grow in balance with its two changing, growing parts.

## Stage Three
## Coinherence: For Better or For Worse

Even at their least intense, consensual sexual relations encourage intimacy, and emotional proximity, particularly that involving physical union, tends toward unification. If prolonged and more than superficial, proximity brings about and fosters a real participation in the other, an indwelling. There is an automatic interpenetration of being which operates, increasing in time to what Charles Williams has dubbed "coinherence."[14]

This semiautomatic process can clearly be seen at work in cases where the relationship is not fully chosen. Cohabiting twosomes, for example, sometimes find that they have become a couple unintentionally, and even against their wishes, and mutually deadening or destructive long-term relationships have been amply documented in recent studies of old age. When cohabitation has been only endured, coinherence still occurs, but its result is either dullness or unresolved conflict,[15] as succinctly illustrated in J. V. Cunningham's epigram on experience as a mistress of longstanding, which concludes wrathfully: "I . . . would kill her, but which of us is which?" or in Sartre's vision of hell in *No Exit*, where three people are locked in an eternally torturing triangle, each by being self-preventing and in turn being prevented from enjoying happiness.

This is not to be equated with the life-giving friction of conflict in couples who learn to "fight fair." If such couples persevere, observing with gentle respect times of greater and lesser intensity, they will proceed onward toward greater and greater union, but never without experiencing some combination of great injustice and petty, cumulative, incorrigible annoyance which must be overcome and forgiven. Each must learn to bind up wounds and bury the irreparable. Each must agree to substitute his or her own love for the wrongs or weaknesses of the other. And each must acknowledge fault or incapacity and accept the love offered.

Those who can pass through this last kind of test, who can achieve reconciliation after betrayal or persevere through the thick and thin everydayness of life, can be said to enter into the third stage of conjugal life. When the couple space achieves duration, coordination, and balance, comfortable companionship and mutual affirmation can allow any remaining defense mechanisms to relax, past resentments to dissolve, and personal weaknesses to be faced and conquered. Each lover's awareness stretches outward toward the other, expanding the being of the beloved, and at the same time serves as reality principle, setting boundaries which bring the other face-to-face with finitude until all the strands of personality can be unified and define true self.

As two mature individuals turn all obstacles into trampolines, and continue in mutual conquest and mutual surrender, whether they choose to walk in lock step, reinforcing each other by doing the same things, or, as is most common, in the syncopation of 3/2 time (*not dif-fi-cult*, my music teacher used to coach me), each with a separate vocation, the miracle which is the good couple will show through, a vital, creative union, an easy, habitual, and real rather than formal or theoretical union of mind, body, and heart. The conventional, secular heart shape is one representation of this, the upper part clearly two, the lower and the whole clearly one. A musical chord is another, two separate notes which by their coordination create something of beauty, and something more than they are alone. Two dancers, as well, become mysteriously more and other. As Yeats said, "How can we know the dancer from the dance?"[17] This couple is the ideal end result of the paradoxical human phenomenon on which conjugal spirituality must be based and out of which conjugal discipline and practice must grow.

# 4

# The Spiritual Phenomenon: Henosis

AS A RESULT of the developments alluded to at the end of Chapter 1, it is now possible to consider whether the human phenomenon of coupledom described in Chapter 3 might not be the locus of a spiritual organism hitherto unrecognized by the theological community. At the base of all spiritual practice lies experience of God which cannot be fully communicated to another. In order to refer to the way in which God connects with our thoughts, actions, and emotions, the systematic theology of "traditional" Christian spirituality has found it useful and necessary to speak of an innermost core where God communicates, a spiritual entity coexisting with the body. Aside from the individual soul, traditional theology recognizes, if barely, a communal soul (or perhaps more precisely spirit) which can serve as the place of contact with the divine, this contact usually occurring through religious leaders and prophets, and in a place set aside for that purpose: the burning bush, the temple or the church.

A drastic reworking of this conceptual scheme must occur before it will be possible to realize a spirituality which reflects conjugal rather than private (or communal) experience. In order to do this, it will be useful to be able to imagine a "conjugal soul," a spiritual "place," comparable to the soul or the temple, where God communicates to those in one-to-one relation.

This is, of course, quite a difficult task. Such an organism — one not coterminous with either of the two private souls of which it is composed and also not the same in kind as the spiritual entity recognized, albeit vaguely, in families, churches, and nations — is totally unknown to the history of spirituality. Although in theory its existence is no more or less problematic than the existence of any spiritual reality, it is much more difficult to imagine than the individual soul, even in its concentrated, archetypal form: the long-term commitment, including physical intimacy. Whereas the immaterial soul can be pictured as a diminutive replica of the human because it is housed in a clearly material body, the invisible conjugal "soul" can only be located in another invisible reality, that of relationship.

For, strictly and literally speaking, there are no organs with which two people, as a unit of two, can hear, feel, or see. Conjugal soul can only have body in the bonding which occurs between two people, the growing "areas of coinherence" that result from their encounters, and the almost tangible reality of "the space between" which a couple creates in the course of long-term closeness and commitment. A pair, as pair, is strictly speaking voiceless and powerless in its relations with the outside world. Counsellors must listen attentively to catch the couple's life as expressed through one or the other of its parts. Compared to the solidity of the soul's body, the reality out of which "two-in-relation" must operate can only be characterized as a kind of deaf and dumb, numb, blind paraplegic with no sense of taste or smell!

The import of this for the spiritual life is clear. Conjugal practice cannot be primarily concerned with the exterior world, which the couple, as couple, can know only "second-hand," through the sensory equipment of one of its two parts. The main field of operation for the couple must lie within. As one Catholic counsellor couple observed, "There is an inverse relationship between social involvement with others and fulfillment in marriage."[1]

Yet this is not the entire truth. Human relations do exist as social, if not as physical, units, and fragile though coupledom might be, the existence of one-to-one relationships is a rock-solid practical and spiritual reality ignored at one's peril. "Two-in-relation" is only paraplegic in appearance. Although a pair has no physical organs, it is not entirely voiceless and powerless in dealing with the outside world. "Two-in-relation" can speak and act in unison when they will to do so, and one half, when animated by a spirit of union, can speak and act for the whole.

Above and beyond this, one-to-one relationships by their very existence continually send out messages about the nature of life and love. Through sheer being a couple makes itself known to the outer world, at worst showing all too clearly the difficulties of proximity, at best radiating the joys of companionship. Therefore, it is important, difficult though the task might be, to recognize the existence of the couple as a significant unit and to name and picture for ourselves its spiritual dimension.

## Imagining the Conjugal Soul

The familiar, "celibate" spirituality envisions individuals as discrete circles moving through life, coming now and then within another's gravitational pull, bumping each other and parting, or drawing together for a time in devotion to some common cause. In this view, individuals, like magnetized steel balls, sometimes interact without essential change, or sometimes give up a portion of their absolute independence to become linked with one another, as soap bubbles when linked together lose their perfect circularity.

A truly conjugal spirituality, however, will take into account not only individuals but also encounter, for even those who bump slightly are to some degree affected. Whenever interaction of any kind occurs, there is change. Each trek up marble library steps removes some imperceptible number of molecules so that the steps are gradually worn away, and the leg and body muscles involved in the climb and descent of the stairs respond to the step's measured solidity with a learning which must be recaptured if we have been lying too long abed. All the more so is change inevitable in human interaction. Whenever humans touch, their operational locus is momentarily displaced from "dead-center" and moved, however slightly, in the direction of "the other."

When the outward pull of attraction becomes strong enough to cause interaction and to create relationship, a new density of being becomes necessary to reestablish the individual's stability in the face of the continual and progressive "de-centering" which is taking place. Relationship, therefore, in reaction to the momentary change of center, calls forth new complexity to counterbalance the weight of that pull from the place where the unattached "soul" lay, toward the desirable other. The inner core of the individual who persists in relationship becomes subtly and over time substantially different from its previous self. In this sense, every soul is a conjugal soul, one which links, a person affected by relation.

Beyond this, however, when bonding occurs, when two through intensity of attraction, length of involvement, or deliberate choice join and share each other's lives, an independent, radically new reality is born, the spiritual reality or "conjugal body" which is the basis for "conjugal soul" in its most fully developed, archetypal form. Each, neither absorbing nor being absorbed, becomes more and more permeable to the other. A substantial interpenetration of being takes place. The circles actually begin to overlap, creating a spiritual reality which is both "I" and "not I," "Thou" and "not Thou," significantly and recognizably both two and one. When a pair goes from closeness to commitment, each comes to be partly other as well as self. It is no longer spiritually accurate to consider one alone, in isolation from the conjugal dimension which pervades it. The soul is only partly other, but that part is integral to the definition of its being. With commitment, conjugal soul in its archetypal form comes into being, and with awareness of that conjugal soul, its spiritual dimension is also "born."

## Its Name

As for naming this "conjugal soul," I have as yet found no better suggestion than the rehabilitation of the Biblical archetype of interpersonal unity from the creation account of Genesis 2:24: the Hebrew *basar echadh*, Greek or Latin *henosis*, the "one-flesh" which was the culmination of God's creative work before the entrance of the spoiler serpent. The "one-flesh" referred to can designate not only the adoptive, more-than-blood kinship established between two persons unrelated by blood ties (already mysterious enough), but also nothing less than the reestablishment of primal unity, restoration of the image of God. Layer upon layer of societal interpretation, however, has identified this metaphor for adoptive kinship and sexual union with the strictures of a kind of marriage and monogamy implying inequality of persons. For many, *henosis* connotes claustrophobia

and can at best be thought of as a lost ideal from the Edenic beginning of time or an unobtainable goal at its far-distant other end.

Nevertheless, "one-flesh" has the advantage of directly paralleling terminology familiar to the history of spirituality. The "one
body" imagery used by Paul has served down through the ages to
refer to the church and the Christian community, and intense, nonphysical "one-soul" relationships are recorded from very early times
by celibate theologians. Augustine, for example, wrote 25 years after
the trauma of a friend's death: "Well has someone said of his friend
that he is half of his soul. For I thought that my soul and his soul
were but one soul in two bodies. Therefore, my life was a horror to
me, because I would not live as but a half."[2] And Gregory of Nazianzen spoke of his lifelong friendship with Basil in the same terms:
"It seemed as though there were but one soul between us, having two
bodies. And if we must not believe those who say that all things are
in all things, yet you must believe this, that we were both in each
one of us, and the one in the other . . ."[3]

In addition, the formula, "two-in-one-flesh," conveys well the
paradoxical nature of coupledom, that deceptively familiar secular reality underlying conjugal soul: dividing yet unifying, comforting but
threatening, simultaneously expanding and limiting. "One-flesh" as a
name for the spiritual organism of the long-term dyad connotes mystery, embodiedness, transcendence, and grounded ecstasy. Despite its
drawbacks, it seems at present the best candidate for the task.

## Its Image

Visual images are if anything even more problematic than verbal ones for conveying the invisible. The traditional picture of "two
people looking outward together in the same direction" that has often
been put forward as the ideal of coupledom does indeed show what
the eye can see of those who have taken up the yoke of relationship
and turned in service toward the world, but this is not a distinctively
conjugal image. All individuals and groups relate to others and are
called to service.

The couple is primarily a community of being rather than a
community of doing. Its first and distinctive task, one which it only

partially shares with the individual and the group, is to establish and maintain that being. As we have seen, no individual can create him or herself in the way that a couple must create its relational unit, and the maintenance of group cohesiveness is a task structurally different from the maintenance of intense, one-to-one relationship. I would like to suggest three visual images which point to distinctively conjugal aspects of relationship — one a sculpture, one a drawing, and one a geometric form — each representing one stage of the couple's spiritual lifestyle.

1. "Unitive glimpse"

The first image draws on both realistic and symbolic representation. It is a configuration seen from time to time on book covers or workshop flyers, and is sometimes referred to "the unitive glimpse." Two solid figures face each other in profile — apart, but creating by their orientation a third reality, a space which is seen to have the shape of a goblet. This drawing graphically suggests the almost tangible reality that comes into being when two persons make themselves available to each other. Their focused, attentive love confers on the space between their profiles a solidity, an identity of its own. Their relationship is thus visibly revealed as a new and independent reality, a receptacle in which the two lives can mingle. In some versions the goblet is clearly a chalice. By consecrating the "space between," the couple declare the relationship a *templum*, a space marked out by seers as the location for observing manifestations of God (*templum* in the root sense is "a space marked out by a seer with his divining rod as a location for his observation . . . later . . . the actual observation . . ."[4]).

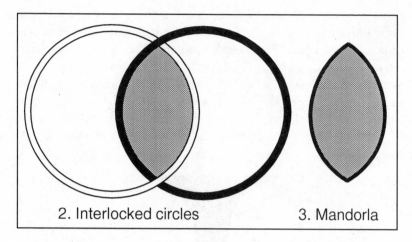

2. Interlocked circles          3. Mandorla

The second image, the interlinked circles used by "Marriage Encounter" groups, uses geometric form to represent both the two distinct parts of the couple and their interpenetration as "one-flesh" over the span of their relationship. Two circles indicate the individual persons, while their overlap shows the substantial effect each has on the other. The oval or ellipse formed by the overlap is uniquely suited, both historically and geometrically, as a symbol for the paradigmatic "conjugal soul."

Historically, it is an ancient ideogram for sexual union, and is also similar to the almond-shaped aureole, or mandorla, enclosing Christ or the Virgin Mary in Eastern Orthodox icons.[5] Geometrically it is fitting because, unlike the circle, it can only be constructed by using two separate points. Its very method of construction, therefore, is "conjugal" and illustrates the dynamics of successful conjugal life.

One can make an ellipse by tying a loose thread between two tacks on a sheet of paper and stretching it outward in all directions with a pencil. There are two, and only two, places absolutely equidistant from both of the centers (just as moments of absolute equality in human relationship are rare). The line from any of the infinite number of other points on its circumference to one of the centers will always be longer than the line to the other (as the benefits of interaction are usually unequal for partners). And as the pencil must proceed through all points on the circumference to form a perfect ellipse, so partners must persevere in relationship, taking turns in getting "the short end" of things, to create harmonious unity out of their duality.

4. "The Kiss"

The final image is Brancusi's long series of nearly identical statues, severely geometrical blocks of granite celebrating the dual life principle, which he produced from 1908 until at least 1937. "The Kiss," as they are all called, is a representation of the close union and fusion of "two-in-one-flesh" which Brancusi, like the Song of Songs and the Book of Revelation, sees as having the power to overcome death. (The original was a funeral sculpture for a Russian girl named Tanosa Gassevskaia in the Montparnasse cemetery in Paris, and is inscribed at the top "the triumph of Love beyond Death.")

The figures are clearly differentiated as two by their hairstyles and by a slight curve indicating the woman's breast; yet equally as clearly, locked in embrace, they suggest one whole cube or rectangle. The lines of their two heads of hair form a single semi-circle of hair when observed from the front, and the profiles of their eyes and mouths meet and appear as one eye and one mouth. The severely stylized compression of the figures — their legs arranged as though squatting and their arms wrapped around the block like a sash — successfully translates into plastic form the physical and emotional union of voluntary and equal coupledom, based on and sustained by the power of sexual attraction and expression.

## Its "Body," Its Modes

Although no image or group of images can capture the full reality of conjugal soul, these three taken together represent more adequately than that portrait of the ideal couple "looking outward together," the cocreated "one-flesh" which, at its fullest, becomes the committed couple. The chalice, the ellipse, and the kiss express in broad outline the almost tangible "space between" of interpersonal mutuality, the symbolic unity of concrete lives, and the mystical union of bodily intimacy. Combining the space between of the chalice, the ovoid area of the interlinked circles, and the fusion of the kiss gives a somewhat adequate idea of the "conjugal soul," which can be dedicated and consecrated as conjugal holy ground.

The specifics of relationship, however, the "body parts" of this invisible reality, are only beginning to be explored. The art of sex has been widely studied, and the use of the space between is now to some degree popularly recognized (some psychologists and counsellors now ask clients to draw appropriately sized and placed circles representing themselves and significant others at different periods in their lives), but a language which would give more flesh to the idea of conjugal soul is still in the process of being articulated, and must still be found before the conjugal way can speak loudly as spiritual discipline.

Maurice Nédoncelle has recently made a contribution in this area by isolating four forms of "We": the "undifferentiated We," identifying with the cosmos or with crowds; the "situational We," in proximities of space and time; the (most important) "functional We," of more closely-knit groups, such as families and communities; and the "personal We" of love.[6]

Ruthellen Josselson has further explored interpersonal reality by identifying eight facets of relatedness, each of which she says is probably at least partly present in everyone's life, but one or two of which usually predominate.[7] The first she describes as "holding," a simple there-ness which provides the secure boundaries which allow being and the groundedness necessary to growth. The second is "attachment," or bonding, which occurs even where the other is incapable of satisfying our needs. The third is the "passion" which longs for union or oneness, the energizer of life and catalyst to self-development. And the fourth is what she calls "eye-to-eye validation," empathy and emotional exchange across space. All of these are primary, being possible from the beginning of life or shortly thereafter.

The other four facets of relation appear after cognitive maturation. Through "idealization" and the process of identifying with another, we transcend the boundaries and limitations of self. Through the resonance of "mutuality," conscious relationship comes into being, the way of experiencing is changed for both, and both carry the one particular relationship into all others. Through "tending" we are responsive to people rather than to principles, and we relate by "embeddedness" to the environments which help shape selfhood.

Each one-flesh pair will experience to greater or lesser degree the longing for union found in "passion" (with the work of conquest and satisfaction of needs which it necessitates), the fidelity of "holding," the comfort of "attachment," tactful "tending" and "embeddedness," the mirroring of "eye-to-eye validation" (which both connects and enables a separate sense of self), and the transcendence of limitation through "mutuality" and "identification" with an idealized other. When concepts such as these become more widely known and used, we can begin to talk with more precision about the "conjugal body" through which the couple as couple experiences God, and about the developing relationship as the principal "place" where couples will look for evidences of God's will, action, and nature.

## Its Motive Force

A special word is in order about the particularity of the love which is the motive force of the closest unit of two, the archetypal conjugal organism. Eros is the energy of the universe, and stands as well behind the human ability to act. Desire is power from within. All our behavior is informed by it. Love is the mysterious, magnetic attraction which leads us to avoid some people and seek others out, to speak or not in the elevator. Involuntary attraction is at the base of all our voluntary relationships (with God, our friends, or loved ones), and it shapes even the ones we cannot choose (our neighbors, teachers, or co-workers), making them harder or easier.

This erotic love is by and large ignored or suspect in our spiritual tradition, however, its physicality until recently held to be (at best) irrelevant to the spiritual life or (at worst) a distraction from the practice of prayer. This is so partly because of a general distrust of the body, but also because eros — including the intense romantic yearning which myth and literature call "falling in love" and the physical act which is sometimes its culmination — is in fact risky, a potential challenge to order and self-control.

Passion can be unreasonable and inconvenient, accidental or unexpected, and sometimes unwanted or harmful. We have little or no control over it, it comes and goes, highly nonrational and potentially illusory. It can even in some cases take the form of a personal response to qualities which remain absolutely invisible to everyone else, a private revelation which cynics, ancient and modern, call "madness." Even in its weakest manifestation the powerful attractiveness of a beloved pulls the self outward in desire and longing, leaving the lover's being open and vulnerable, and there is always the possibility of rejection from the object of admiration.

Yet attraction, desire and longing are spiritually worth the risk, for they force us continually outward to learn the lessons of unity. They break down our ego boundaries, allowing the self to be enlarged and enriched by knowing others, by learning from them and interacting with them. Love acts on the personal level to stretch the boundaries of the soul, enlarging it by effecting a radical openness to the other. Especially when mutual, but even when not, the outflow of love, grounded in sensory and kinesthetic experience and awareness of the other, can at its best give a sense of joy and harmony, culminating sometimes in ecstatic experience in which individuals are totally transformed. (First love is widely recognized as the life experience most likely to turn a person, however fleetingly, into a poet.)

Love as a spiritual discipline, therefore, can pleasurably tempt one toward self-forgetfulness and self-transcendence, so that two persons can meet as "living beings through which divine being may sound (per-sonare)."[8] As the Russian Orthodox priest, Yelchaninov, has pointed out, ". . . a single vivid experience of love will advance us much farther, will far more surely protect our souls from evil, than the most arduous *struggle* against sin."[9] Adoration can lead to the self-offering which makes space (ecstasy is, literally, "standing out from" oneself) for God to come in, for transfiguration.

The recognition of "God" in another, our attraction to this revelation, and the affinity it brings into being are the basis for spiritual friendship as well as for the more intimate conjugal relations. Increase in the ability to see and love value outside the self has always been recognized as a measure of progress in the life of the spirit. The passion of the person who enters into relation, however, is subtly but substantially different from this general eros.

From the relational, conjugal perspective, love is called forth not only by the value perceived in the other but also by value perceived in the association itself. The movement of love from a conjugal perspective, therefore, is not simply centrifugal, moving away from self-centeredness (as is the case in the traditional moral scheme), but also centripetal, revolving around the axis created by its own being, the axis defining two as standing in relation. The primary spiritual task of conjugal love is the creation, maintenance, and growth of that unique reality which is each new relation, the necessary foundation for joint outward-looking service.

In the most highly developed form of conjugal love, couples add the element of duration to the inward attraction felt by individuals and the outward mutuality enjoyed by consensual pairs. They choose to enter into commitments based on the suspicion or guess or wager or hope that the other's particular imperfections are tolerable enough not to spoil the developing affinity or impede interpenetration, and that the other's perfections and one's own will fit together as some sort of whole, will in religious terms reunify divided humanity, thus recreating in some imperfect degree the image of God. The courtly love tradition, though it teaches that love can only last if unfulfilled, has at least that in it of truth that sees the revelation of "the other" as spiritual call and the confirmation of compatibility as holy grail.

The crucial difference between this conjugal love and the "celibate" version of it is that the conjugal most characteristically makes full use of the body. All love is to some degree embodied, whether that is conveyed by body language or not. Whenever attraction occurs, the pulse rate will quicken and the body feel more alive. Erotic experience touches the deepest layers of the spiritual being and can lead to the emergence of profound modes of consciousness.[10] But in the loving erotic relationship, which is cultivated as such and dedicated to God, conjugal love yields a kind of knowledge of the self, the other, and God not obtainable in any other way.

When two bodies are intentionally brought together as one temple for the spirit, lovers "know" as sexual beings. Their bodily intercourse results in the binding of two minds with one thought and leads on to a veritable possession by a power greater and beyond the individuals, a power which displaces recognizable selves by acute physical awareness. Such conjugal interchange, with its taking and giving and its attentiveness to the five senses, provides the ground for the ongoing life of the conjugal soul. Through the fulfillment of desire in sexual union, the couple can experience the presence of the spirit and the possibilities of heaven. What then will be the stages in the ongoing life of this conjugal soul, this spiritual reality seated in the grail of lives?

# 5

# Developmental Stages

BOOKS ON THE COUPLE AND THE SPIRITUAL LIFE speak of varying numbers of steps in their development. Evelyn and James Whitehead see it in outline form, consisting of broad "passages," or transitions: from "I" to "We" (from romance to commitment), and from "We are" to "We care" (from the couple to the world). Susan Campbell defines it as a journey in five phases (romance, power-struggle, stability, commitment, and cocreation), whereas Joan Timmerman speaks of six stages (sexual unfolding-spiritual awakening; making and breaking commitments; commitment in marriage; pregnancy and parenting; loving again after loss; and keeping alive while aging). Betty Bethards (along with others) has convincingly subdivided even further, speaking of seven-year cycles of crisis and renewal (romantic fusion; expectations and compromise; power struggle and control; competition, the seven-year itch; reconciliation and cooperation; and acceptance and collaboration). She proposes conjugal "check-ups" at midcycle to foster growth and the assimilation of growth.

Precise measurements are not of the essence, however. Stages in the spiritual life are never reducible to successive periods of time. They are in any number artificial constructs which serve to give shape and a sense of progress to the natural, rhythmic flow of human life, but can never entirely do justice to its overlapping, backtracking, start-and-stop process. They flow into and mingle with each other, fading and recurring — aspects, really, rather than stages. Nor is value determined by longevity. For while half a century is not too long to explore the infinite phases of love, to try to get to the bottom of unfathomable otherness, it is quite possible, as C. S. Lewis and

Joy Davidman showed, to come to wholeness within a very short space of time.[1]

From a practical point of view, when more information about the spiritual life of couples is available, it may well be found that the seven-year, cyclical model will most adequately describe conjugal reality, its shape spiral rather than vertical, the return of earlier "stages" not regression but lamination, not a step backward but the adding of another, strengthening layer. I have chosen to work with only three divisions, however, which in addition to the virtue of simplicity will also have the advantage of facilitating dialogue with mystical theology, which has traditionally described the spiritual life in three stages: the purgative, illuminative, and unitive; or, in Jean-Jacques Olier's body-based, evolutionary and nonprogressive version: adoration, cooperation, and communion.

The joint life from which a couple's spirituality must emerge can thus be divided into three different stages which are not strictly chronological, but also ongoing and alternating aspects of conjugal existence with the same basic but developing disciplines: a formative phase, lasting up to 14 years or more, in which the couple comes into being and is continually creating its own distinctive chalice shape; a second, long, middle period of consolidation and change, in which it copes with both the ellipsis of the joint life it has created and with the outside world; and finally, those perfect ecstatic moments or periods when the couple achieves and celebrates a joyful, sexual union of mind, body, and heart. These three stages or ongoing tasks — creation, cultivation, and celebration — symbolized by the chalice, the oval, and the kiss, can also be labelled with three words familiar from the second creation account in Genesis — leaving, cleaving, and becoming one-flesh.

## A Different Discipline

The broad theological outlines of the conjugal spirituality and the spiritual discipline proper to the couple were indicated early in the 20th century in the diary of Alexander Yelchaninov, a Russian Orthodox priest who was one of a large group of Russian intelligentsia exiled in Paris. Among his unsystematic musings can be found both a definition of coupledom and a formulation of its particular kind of asceticism. Yelchaninov defines the couple as the mystical union of two beings formed by the two disciplines of renouncing oneself (that is, giving oneself to another) without losing oneself, and by "taking" another ("I take thee to be my . . .") without using the force that kills love.[2] Self-renunciation and nonviolent "taking" create coinherence, or conjugal community, and establish it as kingdom. As couples achieve mastery in this discipline, they undergo gradual but complete personal transformation and acquire a full and unique knowledge of the other, which Yelchaninov says is comparable to the mystic's knowledge of God.

At mid-century the historian and theologian D. S. Bailey, in pondering "the consequences of Man's sexual duality as an image of God," gave more modern definition and specificity to the couple's ascetical task, which he also saw as twofold: the preservation of sexual integrity and the acceptance of sexual partnership.[3] This definition has continued to be used, being echoed recently, for example, by Catholic marriage counsellors Joseph and Lois Bird, who write that the couple's "twofold obligation is to give sexual fulfillment and to strive to achieve it . . ."[4] Bailey's formulation has the virtue of underlining the crucial role of sexuality in conjugal discipline and also of substituting positive wholeness for negative renunciation, but his notion of partnership does not bring out as clearly as Yelchaninov's "kingdom" the dimension of mutual conquest and possession.

In both of these definitions the asceticism of coupledom is related to that of religious tradition. The renunciation in Yelchaninov's definition is perfectly comprehensible to spiritual theology, and Bailey's partnership is closely related to the Biblical concept of covenant. There are many more connections which need to be made, however, between the experience of couples and Biblical or theological orthodoxy, and bridges to be built where gaps exist. To work toward the development of a truly conjugal spirituality, it will be necessary to relate the couple's life more systematically to traditional spiritual theology, drawing on tradition to illuminate the spiritual life of the couple so that the couple's spiritual life can further illuminate the tradition.

The disciplines peculiar to couple as couple, growing out of ecstasy, joint being, and the "space between" — the revelatory "glimpse," the ecstatic kiss, and the holy one-flesh of interlinked lives — will encompass action as well as word. Lois and Joseph Bird define prayer as "the directing of one's thoughts *and actions* (my emphasis) toward God, striving to relate to God and to increase God's presence."[5] Although an extension of prayer as traditionally defined, this is not entirely foreign to tradition. Fasting has often been spoken of as prayer with the body. The word for prayer in the Hebrew Scriptures has its root in action-words, including "to prostrate oneself" and "to caress"[6]; and the Episcopal Prayer Book seems to put action on a par with words in worship by providing an order for celebrating the Eucharist in which only the actions to be used, not the words, are specified (i.e., gather, proclaim, respond, pray, exchange, prepare, make, break, share). Since conjugal discipline includes body, action is necessarily implicated. The criteria for its usefulness as spiritual discipline will be whether or not it promotes the habitual attentiveness to the other and the education of the senses necessary for the perfection of the conjugal soul.

## The Formative Stage — Creation: "Leaving" and "Leaf-ing" for a Kingdom; Olier's "Adoration"

In the traditional "purgative," or beginner's stage, the first part of the discipline is to renounce self, combat sin and cultivate virtue, to eliminate obstacles to spiritual progress, including both attachment to material things and habitual, harmful inner dispositions (in the colorful medieval formulation, the "seven deadly sins": gluttony, lust, avarice, melancholy, anger, boredom, vainglory and pride). "Celibate" (i.e., individual) practices aimed at freeing the self for service and for joy include mental prayer and bodily fasting, poverty and celibacy, physical austerities (exposure to heat and cold, lack of sleep) and mental discipline (reflection on the nature of evil desires and thoughts so as to rid oneself of them). Aside from combatting sin, the traditional first stage also involves active "good works" — cultivating strengths ("virtues") and exercising the ascetic muscles in strong, effective love of self, other, and God. In the medieval schema, the seven spiritual and seven corporal works of mercy (feeding the hungry, clothing the naked, sheltering the stranger, visiting the sick, helping prisoners, burying the dead, and visiting widows and orphans) were prescribed to facilitate growth toward perfection.

The first of the conjugal stages can easily be compared to the first part of the traditional formative stage. There is a clear parallel between the conjugal "leaving of father and mother," which clears the way for the creation of the couple, and the active spiritual effort which prepares the ground for individual development. This conjugal version of renunciation is usually overlooked by spiritual writers, for many reasons. First, conjugal life itself is overlooked. Relationship is in general regarded as incidental, like blue eyes or being raised in Alabama, a secondary or tertiary characteristic rather than essential to an individual's personhood. Second, conjugal asceticism is not easily recognized as such by the unpartnered who have produced most of our spiritual literature. The radical proximity necessary to build the "one-flesh" is hard to imagine for those who have not experienced it. Third, the formation of the couple is sometimes not experienced as renunciation by those involved. It is often accomplished with no difficulty, under the impulse of romantic love and the exhilaration of merging worlds. And fourth, it is often not experienced immediately but in later years.

Nevertheless, though often underrated by celibate and married alike, relationship by its very definition entails renunciation of attachments standing in the way — anything or anybody past, present, or future. For the couple, it is not necessary to "choose" purgation. It is built into the situation. Successfully coupled individuals must continually leave behind the past, the past self, and each succeeding self, should they prove obstacles to union. Proximity is a discipline which requires a not inconsiderable degree of self-mastery, necessitating, as we have seen, accountability and reduced privacy, as well as the radical abrasiveness which arises from time to time when unmatching or unpolished edges meet.

Conjugal unity must be brought about through ever-expanding transcendings of background and being. Katherine Anne Porter refers to marriage as the risky strategy "of surrendering gracefully with an air of pure disinterestedness as much of your living self as you can spare without incurring total extinction."[7] Others have called it "treading the fine line between sacrifice and suicide."[8] Compared to the restrictions and losses which everyone is called upon to accept, such as the giving up of youth and the giving up of our lives in death, conjugal renunciations have a hidden radicality. Old age and death are forced upon us like blood relatives in the normal course of events, but voluntary commitments are contingent on our choice. Couples can escape them if they choose to; therefore they must, exactly like monastics, choose over and over not to do so.

"Leaving," however, is closely related etymologically (and perhaps in essence) to the "leaf-ing" of new, creative growth. In "leaving," two people turn from the world and to each other; but as illustrated in the "unitive glimpse," they thereby create a new reality between themselves. Renunciation is not an end in itself but a means to allow participation in God's continuing creativity. Conjugal practice, as well as celibate, involves not only going out *from* self but also going out *for* self, in this case more specifically for self-in-relation. The first stage is not only "purgation" but also pilgrimage: a pilgrimage to find or to make the particular way to which one is called: the "word" (for the individual) or the "dialogue" (for the couple) which will embody God.

Since the goal of conjugal spirituality is not the perfection of person but the perfection of relation, the "leaf-ing" of its first stage is not good works but the creation of the couple. "Good works" in conjugal terms are those acts which foster the formation of the couple, that "container or alchemical vessel in which . . . natures are steadily refined through the heat of . . . proximity and daily interaction."[9] Asceticism for "leaf-ing" thus includes, in addition to those "celibate" disciplines which the individuals adapt and use for themselves, a set of parallel conjugal practices which could be called con-*templ*-ation. Two become one temple for the spirit by continually reaching out, dedicating time, space, and energy to comprehend the presence of God which is in the other and to become aware of the presence of God in their verbal communication and corporal communion. The first and only tool for this building of the one-flesh, as well as for the maintaining and celebrating of it which follow, is that of verbal and nonverbal intercourse, of dialogue and sex, the prayer in action of daily encounter, periodic stocktaking, and regular celebration.

The development of talk as a spiritual exercise for couples dates at least back to mid-century France, when a concerted effort to find spiritual disciplines for the couple was taking place. The primary one which emerged from the search was given the rather ungainly name of *le devoir de s'asseoir*, literally translated "the duty to sit down." The *devoir de s'asseoir*, consisted in setting aside regular times for uninterrupted conversation with one's partner: ten minutes a day, once a week, a monthly retreat. From this basic form, many systems evolved. The earliest model of simple, scheduled conversation was varied, becoming sometimes informal and spontaneous, sometimes planned in subject, sometimes framed by scripture and verbal prayer. Marriage Encounter added the written to the spoken word, along with the individual reflection that this allowed. Many self-help books are now available for training in this discipline.

There are three common objections to considering conjugal dialogue a spiritual exercise or prayer. The first is that it is only a "secular" activity, not "religious." And certainly couples have by and large had to turn to secular disciplines, such as psychology and sociology, to learn the techniques of good one-to-one communication. But talk, like any other human activity, can be dedicated and designated to serve religious purpose. According to a source which I can no longer locate, even bowling was practiced as spiritual exercise by the monks of one medieval European abbey. As William Johnston pointed out in relation to transcendental meditation, biofeedback, and mind control, "Whatever develops human potential should also develop Christian faith, provided this faith is alive and nourished by scripture and liturgy . . ."[10] Just as personal and corporate prayer link the inner word of experience to the outer word of expression, so must conjugal prayer come out of that dialogue which makes up its joint being.

The second objection, following from the first, is that talking "comes naturally," that it is easy (i.e., not a skill to be learned) and pleasurable (i.e., not serious). Yet, as was mentioned in Chapter 2, and as the multiplicity of self-help books on relationship testify, using talk to create intimacy is not always easy and sustaining dialogue over a period of time never comes naturally. In the long run, as with traditional prayer, discipline and skill-learning are necessary.

And finally, some would discount conjugal dialogue because they consider it a subdivision of the individually and communally spoken words of traditional spirituality. Yet, as we have seen, this is at most a partial truth. The words spoken between two alone are radically different from words spoken alone or to more than one. The partner is an immediate and unavoidable sounding board. There is an intensity not possible with more than two and a direct mutuality which even in unequal relationships creates a kind of equality. There is no third to be a tie-breaker; and harmony must be established through sheer inventiveness and perseverance.

Conjugal dialogue intentionally dedicated is thus both valid as spiritual exercise for the couple and distinct from other forms of verbal prayer or worship. Words do not always lead to harmony, however, and there is, in addition, more to communication than talk. Much of relationship is nonverbal encounter, and conjugal strength requires building on acts as well as on words. Those who have difficulty conceiving of talk as spiritual exercise have even more difficulty with action. I recall the question of a Presbyterian minister friend who asked, "What does God care if I mow my lawn?" in much the same way that early writers asked "What has Athens to do with Jerusalem?"

But actions, like words, have meaning: breathing plays an important role in the *Way of a Pilgrim*; Evdokimov calls the mastery of sex "moral theology"; and there is a model for prayer in the midst of activity in the example of Brother Lawrence, whose kitchen duties did not disturb his absorption in God. In the Jewish tradition, there is even precedent for sexual relationship as prayer: there is a Hasidic tradition that David and Bathsheba teach prayer; and there is the story of the Talmudic scholar discovered under his rebbe's be who, upon being discovered and challenged, replied: "It is Torah and I need to learn!"

Among contemporary spiritual directors as well, there is growing acceptance of the idea that action can be prayer. Slade, whose community is founded on that principle, points out that many young people have their first transfiguring experience in some kind of physical movement.[11] Carroll and Dyckman write: "We play constantly before the face of God . . . Sometimes we . . . place ourselves immediately before that loving presence, but that is only to rediscover the truth of a presence that pervades everything. And so all the activities of life . . . can be seen as prayer . . . "[12]

Some recent spiritual writers, benefiting from the accumulating experience of couples, have deemphasized and even cautioned against word-based conjugal practice, recommending instead a regular, pleasurable activity requiring the cooperation of both partners: getting outdoors, exercising, being around happy, creative people, watching kids play in the park or people at the shopping center, or finding a new creative project.[13] Gardening or sex can also be "words" in the conjugal dialogue, strengthening bonds as tightly and revealing God as surely as words can do. Whereas celibates, vowed to chastity, depend heavily on a verbal canon for communion with God and cohesion with each other — Bible reading, the Opus Dei, the Breviary — the body and its activity is the best book for the one-flesh.

The most distinctive of conjugal disciplines and the one least talked about within our churches is sex, the physical act which can become spiritual experience through mutual love and dedication to each other and to God. Like talk in that it is both easy and difficult, natural and to be learned, sex is the most mysterious and the most suspect of all the elements of conjugal spirituality.

Yet ecstatic sexual union, long recognized by the Kabbalists as bodily prayer, is called in *The Westminster Dictionary of Christian Spirituality* the most sacred of human events. Modern research has demonstrated that "every change in physiological state is accompanied by an appropriate change in one's mental and emotional state, conscious or unconscious, and, of course, vice versa."[14] Though I have seen no spiritual writer mention it, such drastic physiological change as sexual orgasm cannot help but have long-term effect on body and therefore on soul, even as other postures and movements, fasting and vigils are known to do within the tradition.

Sexual union begins as a function of two personalities, a singlehearted expression of relatedness and love, but on the edge of ecstasy lovers are totally transformed, becoming totally unlike themselves in any other setting. As Carla Needleman describes it, sexual passion, by displacing the recognizable self, leaves space for "a force, organic and of compelling power, that acts through us and for a short period of time and changes us into beings quite different from the way we are all the rest of the time . . ."[15]

When summoned by that untamable power, if the couple can surrender to its ecstatic joy, harmony, union, and wholeness, they become they know not what. Some speak kataphatically of the presence of Christ. Some, experiencing the suspension of all their exterior senses, the temporary annihilation of time, multiplicity, and corporality, speak of an apophatic, mystical cloud of unknowing. On particularly graced occasions, and progressively over time, a God-like fusing takes place which temporarily transcends duality of being, making the couple more and more a perfect unity, their disparate parts fitting together like Brancusi's perfect cubic couple, a human equivalence, an earthly image of union within the Godhead.

The complete physical and emotional proximity of sexual intercourse — the single most important factor in the creation of the couple's unity — deeply, irrevocably, and continually alters the people involved. It is important, therefore, even though our culture makes that difficult, for couples to study it seriously and to practice it assiduously. It is this sacrificial (i.e., "holy-making") action, the discipline peculiar to conjugal lovers, that above all can make the couple, albeit momentarily, a spiritual one-flesh unit capable of receiving what Brother Pierre-Yves of Taizé so calmly calls *les petites surprises du Saint Esprit,* the little surprises of the Holy Spirit.

## Parallels and Sources in the Tradition

> *It is not good that man should be alone. (Gen. 2:18)*
>
> *When he understood that she was kin, he fell so deeply in love with her that he could no longer call his heart his own. (Tob. 6:18)*

The first part of conjugal discipline, "leaving," can easily adapt the familiar disciplines of "renunciation." The second, creative aspect of this first stage, however, the "leaf-ing," is only obliquely reflected in the tradition. Its closest parallel is to be found in those "one-soul" friendships spoken of by Augustine and Gregory of Nazianzen, and later written about by Aelred — friendship as a means of learning the love of God and of going to God.

Although "one-soul" relationships have historically been discouraged as detrimental to the harmony of the monastic community as a whol, monks, like all human beings, have frequently participated in relations based on attraction and affinity, sometimes even lifelong, and celibate writers have experienced growing together so intimately in thought and feeling with another that they form "one spirit in two bodies."

But "one-soul" is substantially different from "one-flesh." Monastic vows of celibacy rule out the kind of total commitment to another and the kind of total union of lives which permits the fullest development of conjugal spirituality. The couple must look to other parts of the tradition to find itself fully reflected.

Since physical closeness and full coinherence are totally absent from the mainline classics of Christian spirituality, it is only by going outside monastic tradition that one can find fully consonant models for conjugal "self-with-other." One can look to Judaism, for example, which has always acknowledged the couple and their joining as a spiritual event. The 13th-century *Holy Letter ('Iggereth Hakodesh)* teaches that whenever two lovers of God unite in thought and deed, the Shekinah (God's presence in the world) rests between them.[16] It describes in six chapters "the way in which a man may consummate sexual union with his wife so that it will be for the sake of heaven,"[17] a way in which the couple is of one mind and heart in arriving at their goal, and in which the divine presence is manifest.

The Talmudist and Kabbalist Nachmanides (1194-1270), a rabbi and a physician, taught that God was with the male and female in sex, that sex was not only pure but holy, and that couples at the Last Judgment would be called to account not only for their sins but also for all the legitimate pleasures which they had failed to enjoy.[18] This approach to the sexual is typical of the "Thou shalt" model reflected in rabbinical tradition. Sexual intercourse was a religious discipline enjoined in the Law, to be performed every day by the unoccupied, once a week by ass-drivers, once in 30 days by camel-drivers, and at least once in six months by sailors.[19]

The strength of this position may show through even in the aggressively celibate Paul. Some rabbinical authorities allowed abstinence from sexual intercourse even without the wife's consent, thus disrupting conjugal community, if the purpose was to study the Law: one week for laborers, 30 days for disciples.[20] Paul, on the other hand, despite the urgency he felt in "these present times of stress" (I Cor. 7:26), expecting the imminent end of the world, makes no such exception for preaching the gospel. On the contrary, he advises that married couples "not refuse each other except by mutual consent, and then only *for an agreed time* (my emphasis)" (I Cor. 7:1-7).

Paul's words advising that couples abstain from sex "to leave themselves free for prayer" are often understood to imply that sex, even if conjugal, is an obstacle to the spirit, and that couples should be encouraged to abstain from a purely human activity and turn to the really important "religious" activity of prayer. Even Donald Goergan, for example, writes that "his (Paul's) main concern is that their sexual life not get in the way of their prayer life."[21]

In the light of the rabbinical tradition with which Paul was fully familiar, however, it is possible (though possibly "heretical"!) to say that Paul's words mean, or at least imply, that the two activities, individual prayer and conjugal intercourse, are of parallel and equivalent importance, sexual intercourse in an ongoing relationship being the normative conjugal spiritual discipline. "Everybody has his own particular gifts . . ." (I Cor. 7:7). If this interpretation is not correct, then it would seem that one partner could in theory entirely prevent the other from "praying" by withholding consent!

At any rate, human pairs and their problems are prominent in Hebrew and Christian scripture from beginning to end, from the figures of Adam and Eve in Genesis through the polygamous patriarchs and their realistic conjugal predicaments, the married and unmarried prophets and apostles with their imagery and advice, down to the symbolic union of the Spirit and the Bride in the Book of Revelation. Even the lawgiving portions of the Old Testament reflect the primacy of the couple: the soldier was exempt from military duty for one year after marriage; and at a time when women were on the whole little more than property, the law delivered on Mt. Sinai commanded the honoring of both father and mother.

The Biblical evidence as a whole suggests in a number of ways that the human-in-harmonious-relation is our most reliable clue to the nature of God. Genesis uses the same words ("image" and "likeness") about God's creating and human begetting. (In 1:26 we read "God said: Let us make man in our own image, in the likeness of ourselves," and in 5:3, "Adam . . . became the father of a son, in his likeness, as his image. . . .") Likewise, the same Hebrew word, *toledot*, is used for God's days of work and the human family tree, for creation and procreation. ("These are the generations of the heavens and the earth when they were created," (2:4) and "This is the book of the generations of Adam" (5:1).)

Going beyond linguistic linkages to suggestions contained within narrative, Phyllis Trible has pointed out that in the creation account God disappears as soon as the closeness of one flesh is established, not speaking or acting again until disharmony is sown by the serpent and must be dealt with.[22] The narrative thus suggests that human beings will at best be stand-ins, or visible purveyors of God's presence when all goes well, when they are in harmonious relationship. The God of salvation may need to make an appearance in human affairs, but the God of creation rests and enjoys as humankind, the reflected image and likeness, carries on two by two. There are indeed long stretches of the Bible where there is no overt divine intervention, where God acts through the *imago* ("and let them be masters . . ." 1:26). Conjugal being, like the whole people of God, is formed by a movement of exodus from the known to the unknown, a call to participate in God's creativity and action in the world.

There is, in addition to the verbal evidence of the Bible, a visual model which echoes the chalice of the "unitive glimpse" and integrally links the couple to the presence of God. The cherubim in the Bible were representations of the two spiritual beings overshadowing the place where Yahweh first "dwelt with" the people, in the middle of the Holy of Holies of the first temple at Jerusalem. A fairly detailed description of their setting is given in three places in the Hebrew scriptures (Ex. 25:18, I Kg. 6:23-28, and II Kg. 3:10-13).

The two cherubim stood on the ends of the ark of the covenant which had been carried by the Hebrews throughout their desert wanderings, a small portable box or chest of acacia wood overlaid with gold, inside and out. Its top was a gold plate called the *kapporet*, the "propitiatory" or "mercy seat," and at the ends of this ark-cover, of one piece with it, stood the golden cherubim facing each other, their wings overshadowing the throne of mercy. "There," Yahweh said, "I shall come to meet you; there, from above the throne of mercy, from between the two cherubs that are on the ark of the Testimony I shall give you all my commands for the sons of Israel (Ex. 25:22)." More than once, as in I Sam. 4:4, Yahweh is referred to as "He Who is enthroned upon the cherubim." God's earliest sustained self-revelation thus came from a space created by the bodies of the cherubim, two equal beings oriented toward each other, their wing tips touching over the place of presence.

It is possible that these cherubim are present, though not explicitly, in the Christian tradition as well. If they are assumed to have remained an integral part of the ark-top/mercy-seat/throne, this Jewish setting for divine theophany reappears, but brought out from the inner sanctuary for all to see, in the last book of the Christian scriptures. The "throne of God and of the Lamb," from which rises the river of life, has its place in the holy city coming down from heaven for the final union of human and divine ("The throne of God and of the Lamb will be in its place in the city," Rev. 22:3-5).

A hint of the cherubim also survives in the symbolic language of Christian iconography. The almond-shaped aureole or mandorla enclosing Christ, the Virgin Mary, or other images of holiness recalls by its oval shape the space created by their bodies and wings. Thus, in what the *Holy Letter* calls the "mystery of the cherubim,"[23] in what Revelation (1:7) may refer to as "God's secret intention," and Tobit (12:7), "the secret of a king," celibate couples form one-soul frames for the deity, and conjugal couples one-flesh, their lives recapitulating the pilgrimage of the Biblical patriarchs. As the cherubim turned from the world to each other, couples "leave father and mother" to create new space for God.

## The Transformative Stage — Cultivation: "Cleaving"; Olier's "Co-operation"

In the middle, "proficient," or "illuminative" stage of traditional mysticism, the spiritual achievements and discoveries of the first stage are focused, consolidated and strengthened. The soul, having acquired some experience of the spiritual journey and some existential knowledge of the fruits which are its goal, proceeds to mobilize these discoveries in order to grow further in love.

The conjugal version of this stage of the spiritual journey is also a mobilization and cultivation of discoveries, but one which can by definition have no exact equivalent in the celibate tradition. In the conjugal second stage, the couple must use the wisdom and knowledge it has acquired and the unity it has experienced to maintain its relationship in being. It does this by fostering the kind of whole-to-whole relatedness which leads to growth through mutual interpenetration. As recognized by theologians as diverse as Charles Williams and Peter Baelz, when mind, body, and spirit relate fully to another mind, body, and spirit, the increasing interpenetration of being which results becomes a spiritual unit distinct from the two individuals. The "conjugal soul," the ground for a dual, conjugal relationship with God, constitutes the springboard for a joint communing or uniting with, imitating or participating in divine being which will allow joint growth in love.

In the first stage, the couple learned the tight-rope routine of "treading the fine line between sacrifice and suicide," discovering which actions on their high-wire would allow movement without causing either to fall. In the second, renunciation and creation are supplemented by the courage to continue widening the self, curious probing to understand the spark of divinity in the other, and patient prioritizing to maintain the equilibrium which has been achieved. Practice and pluck must join creativity to deal with the complications of growing interpenetration and the balancing of the "I-You-We" triad with the fourth dimension "They" of other commitment. Juggling must be added to the balancing act. The couple must flexibly pass through all the points necessary to form the perfect oval of their elliptical holy space, must hear their own voice and the other's and modulate to form the perfect chord.

The couple enters this second stage of conjugal development when they realize that their relationship has not only become a reality, but a reality with a history. The second is the longest of the stages, and its task of incorporating and harmonizing the changes taking place within and between the individuals is the most difficult. It is to this stage that Holmes is primarily referring when he describes conjugal discipline as the balancing of partnership and integrity.

As was the case in the formative stage, one aspect of the conjugal discipline at this stage seems at first glance more familiar than the other. Achieving and maintaining integrity would seem to be a task common to all. But the similarity is only partial. Since the coupled person on principle has chosen to be an "I-Thou," has chosen, on principle, to be permeable, all relationships, actions, thoughts and feelings are to some degree affected by this complication. Integrity for a couple is different from individual integrity, and more difficult. Coupled individuals in a sense take on duality of being, and each individual act impacts not only their own being but also their joint existence, health, and development.

The second aspect of conjugal discipline at this stage, long-term transfiguration, or growth in partnership, is (like the creation of the one-flesh in the first stage) more obviously different from its "celibate" analogue. The couple grows primarily not by detachment but by attachment, learning to increase similarities and tolerate differences with the other. Each partner affects the other for good or for ill within the safe or stifling space created by their mutual choosing and choices. Safe space can only be maintained and nourished by continual loving contact. Through encounter each is challenged and expanded, consciousnesses gradually enlarged. Each can be gently nudged when God seems absent, so that both arrive at the fullest possible humanity, learning to give and to take, to nurture and to achieve. Lovers must become expert in breaking down barriers and persist in attempting to "conquer" the inaccessible, the inexhaustible, ultimately unknowable other, to make a more perfect "fit."

The second-stage disciplines with which these tasks are accomplished are continuous with the ones by which the relationship was first created. Lovers must still use ears, eyes, confrontation, humor, praise and affirmation, negotiation and balance, passion and leisurely lovemaking. But in the second stage it is no longer a question of learning these skills but of practicing and mastering them, of perfecting, in Evdokimov's words, "the inventive art of the greatest love,"[24] the *magnus amor*.

What was spontaneous becomes cultivated, intentional, and even ritual. After a given level of familiarity is attained, verbal exchange becomes less frequent because less necessary, partly replaced (as occurs in the development of individual prayer) with an intuitive communion beyond words. To get more deeply into what is there, therefore, talk at this stage should be ritualized, conscious and regular. The couple should institute appointments or dates, as from the early days, to keep lines of communication open and to keep up with the changes going on in each other's lives. The skills of listening and empathizing must be honed, seeing the world from the other's point of view while still keeping one's own identity and objectivity. Conflict must be recognized as a stimulus to reestablish balance when things are "out of whack," as normal, life-giving friction which can restore warmth and sensitivity, as a way to learn diplomacy and to prevent stoppage and stagnation (thus the spiritual movement called "Marriage *Encounter*"), and ultimately, therefore, as a means to truth.

In addition, couples must continually break new ground around their holy space. They must from time to time get away from ordinary life by taking a retreat. Church-sponsored weekends are sometimes scheduled, but even holing up at home for a day, "snowed in," turning off the telephone and drawing the curtains is passable. Marriage Encounter weekends, widely available across denominational lines, offer a fixed and well-thought-out progression of lectures by lead couples, alternating with structured sharing within the dyads, leading toward closure.

The need for renewal and exploration applies particularly in the area of sex. Throughout life, time should be taken for the education of the senses, the couple's gateway to God. Both should explore various physical disciplines and meditative techniques, apart and together, to exercise the body. Sensory awareness and yoga strengthen and delight the conjugal as well as the individual soul, and the erotic disciplines peculiar to sexual activity likewise fill the conjugal soul with joy and give it vigor and long life.

## Parallels and Sources in the Tradition

> *"Am I not more to you than ten sons?" (I Sm. 1:2)*
>
> *"In the night my loins instruct me." (Ps. 16:7)*

The Biblical term "cleaving" is particularly appropriate as a designation for the discipline of this second stage in which couples daily link their lives to maintain the sacred space created. The word itself has seemingly contradictory meanings, which correspond to the two seemingly contradictory disciplines necessary to healthy ongoing relationship: uniting with another and yet establishing boundaries which exclude the other. ("To cleave" means both "to separate," as in the word "cleaver," and "to attach oneself closely to," in both the physical and the metaphorical sense.) In addition, the Bible uses "cleaving" to refer specifically to human love. In the Hebrew scriptures, cleaving covers the whole gamut from friendly affection to passionate desire; and in the Christian, with the intensity of its eschatological focus, cleaving is primarily that staple of conjugal discipline, the sexual intercourse which expresses sexual love.

Within theological tradition the model discipline for conjugal second-stage practice could be the *imitatio Dei*, the imitation of God. "We all, with unveiled face, beholding the glory of the Lord, are being changed into his likeness from one degree of glory to another" (II Cor. 3:18). For the couple specifically, however, the likeness to be imitated is not that of the historical Jesus or that shown in Michelangelo's picture of God creating Adam, but that of Rublev's mutually-gazing Trinity: not God in exterior relation, but God as harmoniously relational mutuality of being. The intradivine relationship is pictured in Rublev's icon as three angelic figures in close association with the couple. The tower and tree in the background stand in the place of Abraham and Sarah, the original hosts in Biblical and iconographic tradition. The three angels, though three and apart, have many affinities with Brancusi's statue. They are static figures, fitting with ease into a geometric shape, in this case, an almost circular oval. They are substantially the same in hair, wings, staffs and faces, and slightly but clearly differentiated by minor variations in their clothing and position. And they are clearly oriented one to the other, willing thus to be eternally joined.

There is also ample imagery from the wisdom literature of the Bible to support second-stage conjugal spirituality. As the first stage resonated with themes of genesis and exodus, the transformative stage corresponds to the annals of conquest and kingdom. Humans, not divine intermediaries, are God's agents. Prosperity, happiness and long life are divine blessings, and human wisdom and skill evidence of divine action.

Solomon, the king allowed to build Yahweh's temple, is granted "immense wisdom and understanding, and a heart as vast as the sand on the seashore," along with a genius for literary creativity (3,000 proverbs and 1,005 songs) and encyclopedic knowledge of plants, animals, birds, reptiles, and fish (I Kg. 5:9-13). The skill of his workmen also is a gift of God: "See, I have singled out Bezalel son of Uri, son of Hur, of the tribe of Judah. I have filled him with the spirit of God and endowed him with skill and perception and knowledge for every kind of craft . . . Here and now I give him a partner, Oholiab son of Ahisamach, of the tribe of Dan; and to all the men that have skill I have given more, for them to carry out all that I have commanded you . . ." (Ex. 31:1-6).

Guiding angels do appear in the story of Tobit to bring together lovers separated by distance and obstacles, and to provide a cure for a righteous man stricken with blindness; but references to God are occasional in the Davidic chronicles and scarce in books like Proverbs. The book of Ruth unrolls with Yahweh in the background, and God appears only as a most vehement flame in the appendix to the lovers' dialogue in the *Song of Songs*.

Aside from general content of the Bible, however, the symbolism of the curious covenant rite used to reassure a dubious Abraham that he would be given the promised land suggests an image to represent the process of the second stage development. The word "cleaving" in the Bible usually refers to earthly realities — the creation of a safe space (e.g., scales tightly spaced on the crocodile or closely soldered onto a breastplate) or the close association of two separate things (as a sword in the hand). In one very early occurrence of it, however, cleaving appears in addition as the divinely ordained preparation for an action of God.

In the account of Genesis 15:1-21, Abraham, doubting but following God's command, ritually splits the designated animals and arranges them symmetrically on an improvised altar before falling into a deep sleep (reminiscent of the creation/separation of the sexes in chapter two in Genesis). God then, in the guise of a firebrand (recalling the "most vehement flame" of the Song of Songs), passes in the space between the separated halves, to signify that he will manage, even through the separated pieces, to assure to Abraham coupledom, fruitfulness, peace, and long life. The separation effected by a human being is symbolically reversed by divine reassurance. Balanced halves again, as with the cherubim in the temple, provide the setting for theophany. God is present "in between" and "for" pairing.

## Dark Night

*"Properly used, marriage like a verse form creates impasses which ask for patience, forbearance, and inspiration." (Wendell Berry)*

*"Courage! Stand firm, and you will see what Yahweh will do to save you . . ." (Ex. 14:13, Moses answering the people).*

Traditionally, entry into the last stage of the spiritual life is through an experience called the "dark night of the soul," a purification in which the soul's devotion is perfected by the withdrawal of all sense of consolation, reward and even sometimes hope. The soul no longer experiences the presence of God or feels that it has any knowledge of God.

The conjugal soul experiences its own version of "the dark night." Indeed, foretastes of it recur throughout the earlier stages in conjugal development. From time to time, the couple runs into a period of "stalemate" which causes it to lose its vision and be tossed into disequilibrium. Couples who persevere in relationship, however, eventually recognize that these dimmings and resurrections of the original vision, like "aridity" and "consolation" within the Ignatian tradition, are normal fluctuations which do not threaten their existence and its relationship to God.

Yet sometimes great injustices or betrayals occur which take away all sense of that relationship, and more clearly correspond to the total desolation of the "dark night." These require transcendent courage in the face of God's most fearsome manifestation, and transcendent acts of creativity and forgiveness. If love can persist, accept and be accepted in these periods, extreme suffering can mark the threshold of a new stage and new gifts, the final stage of conjugal perfection, corresponding to the unitive mystical state.

## The Unitive Stage — Celebration
## "Swiving" Olier's "Communion"

Mystical union with God is a transcendent state of joyful vitality which is sometimes referred to as deification, and which is associated with the notion of sainthood. Though the practices of earlier stages are often continued, contemplation, with "spiritual marriage" as its highest degree, is most characteristic of this period. The soul knows God, knows itself in God, and acts in loving harmony with that knowledge. The unitive is a celebratory stage in which, according to Guigo II, there is constant awareness of God's presence and habitual conformity to God's will.

In the conjugal equivalent, the couple that has reached the unitive state becomes finally and fully aware of God's presence in their joint relationship, and lives in joyous celebration of that knowledge which earlier was only fleetingly available to them. Transfigured in mind and senses by their practice of con-templ-ation, by the graceful inhabiting of joint spiritual space, the couple through the long-term practice of unity becomes a bodily incarnation of that "perpetually renewed contentment, new gushing forth of love, and ever-new embrace within the Unity"[25] which, according to Ruysbroeck, is the mutual life of the Godhead. In the unitive conjugal as in the unitive celibate stage, this love radiates outward. The couple becomes a visible dwelling place for God as Trinity. As Eckhart put it, as the human becomes "God-kin," the couple becomes "Godhead-kin."

This conjugal saintliness is clearly an ideal from which most of what we see and experience is far removed. But just as clearly our perceptions of ourselves and of others are drastically limited by what we expect to see, as a French wine expert discovered when he misidentified as a cheap Spanish vintage an excellent white wine that had been colored red without changing the taste. If there are couplesaints around, we might not even recognize them, and if we have never looked for the work of the Spirit in sexuality, we probably haven't noticed it. Besides, saints are rare, and holy couples should be statistically rarer still. Logically, one could expect a three-to-one ratio, since there are not only two human beings but their relationship to perfect.

Because conjugal saints are so few and so invisible, and because there is so little written about the lives of successful long-term couples, and even less about the spiritual significance of their lives, it is simplest at this rudimentary stage of our knowledge to focus, for comparison with the celibate tradition, on something for which more data is more publicly available: celibate and conjugal ecstasy as emblematic foretastes of their respective unitive stages and as celebratory, symbolic recapitulations of the human-divine relationship.

It is a generally acknowledged fact, even within the historical tradition, that there are substantial areas of overlap between mystical and sexual ecstasy. Both have been described as extreme and irresistible experiences in which one is beside oneself, the exterior senses inoperative. Both have been described as ineffable, fluctuating in intensity, transient, and not reproducible at will, and both noted for their transcendence of time and space, subject and object, within and without, their surrender to an overwhelming power, and their outcome in non-rational and unitive knowledge.[26] The sexual, like the mystical, sets aside a special time and space, transforms the ordinary consciousness, and leads to an increase in freedom to act in love.

On the phenomenological level, traditional and sexual ecstasy are remarkably similar. There are only three elements in a traditional definition of ecstasy (such as that of Poulain) which are absent from that list of commonly mentioned similarities: knowledge of God as the content of the experience, virtue as its context, and a religious subject as the mind's focus.[27] Two of these three can be demonstrated in the conjugal practice described in the writings of contemporary Christians, such as Joseph and Lois Bird.

The presence of the first and second of Poulain's three elements is affirmed by the Birds, who testify to experiencing God within the context of their sexual intercourse. The marital union, according to Joseph and Lois Bird, is a profound prayer, a channel of grace through which husband and wife gradually become aware of Christ's presence as they grow toward mutual sanctity, and a glimpse of the beatific vision.[28] "When we speak of finding Christ in the marital union, we are talking about a personal encounter. It is an emotional experience of a spiritual nature which accompanies the lovemaking in a mature marriage . . . The more we are present for each other, the more He is present to us."[29] Priest and sociologist Andrew Greeley, perhaps echoing them, also affirms that "the greater the pleasure . . . the more is God present . . . ."[30]

They report, moreover, that their experience is not unique, that many other well-regarded Christian couples have spoken to them of orgasm as a moving spiritual experience.[31] Spiritual experience in the context of sexual union is thus validated by the testimony of these virtuous and fruitful lives. The third element, however, the requirement that the mind be focused on a religious subject, is in need of adaptation to make it apply to couples. Though couples can in theory experience the same presence of Christ or be caught up in the same cloud of unknowing as the celibate mystics, the conjugal path to union is so different as to need "translation" before its equivalence to individual prayer can been seen.

There are two major differences — one that it is a dual path, and the other that it passes through the activity of the senses rather than through the contemplative mind. There are "minds," plural, in relation to God, rather than "mind," singular, and not only "minds," but whole persons. The body remains for some a barrier to the acceptance of sexual relating as religious discipline. Achtemeier denies that knowledge of God can be communicated in sex,[32] and Dessesprit writes that no correlation is possible between mystical and sexual ecstasy.[33] In order to affirm that sexual ecstasy can convey knowledge of God, Poulain would doubtless require these two questions to be dealt with: whether mystical encounter with God may be jointly experienced, and whether the spirit can speak through sexual relation.

Dual mystical experience is decidedly an odd idea at first, but it is not entirely unknown in the history of spirituality. The most famous example is that of the vision at Ostia in which joint contemplation leads to vision, proving that mind plural as well as mind singular can know God. The passage describing the experience is particularly powerful because Augustine not only conveys a sense of the (ultimately inexpressible) mystical experience which he and Monica share, but in a sense shares it with the reader as well by skillfully providing a vicarious experience of its mystery and power.

Their meditation, which immediately precedes the joint experience of God, has been focusing on admiration of God's work on earth, in heaven, "higher yet" in their minds, then finally, leaving behind all God's works, admiration of the "region . . . where life is that Wisdom (Christ) by which all these things are made . . ." The "vision" of God is then narrated, or rather adumbrated, in two sentences which impart a sense of it by using metaphorical language. "And while we spoke of the eternal Wisdom, longing for it and straining for it with all the strength of our hearts, for one fleeting instant we reached out and touched it. Then with a sigh, leaving our spiritual harvest bound to it, we returned to the sound of our own speech in which each word has a beginning and an ending."[34]

In this passage Augustine speaks of inner, spiritual sense organs at work in him and in his mother simultaneously, reaching out and touching God. Then, seeming to continue his narration, he indirectly suggests that the active "touching" elicited a communicative "word" from God which, unlike their own finite words, was without beginning or end. That God "spoke" is not stated but suggested after the fact by implied contrast with the human words. The reader must retrospectively reconstruct this information at two removes, realizing first that some fruitful communication which was not narrated has taken place, and then making the effort to conceive its possibility, to imagine speech magnified to such an infinite degree, to the absolute.[35] Augustine and Monica, accompanied by the reader, thus go out and return in joint activity, unity of purpose, and common goal.

Dual "mind" can thus accede to God. But can the whole person? The predominant answer within our tradition has been "no." It has by and large been traditionally assumed that mystical ecstasy can occur only from within the mental realm, and is fostered only by the will and the rational faculties. In the celibate experience of rapture, the mind focuses on a religious object, progressively stills and silences the physical senses, and is finally itself overwhelmed by an extraordinary inflow of the spirit, sometimes experienced as an operation of spiritual senses paralleling the physical ones, sometimes as a cloud of unknowing. Ecstatic progress is thus incrementally measured by the regression of sensual awareness and activity.

Thus if, as is the case in sexual activity, the senses should overthrow the mind before mind can itself be overthrown by spirit, there would be no ground left in which the spirit could take hold and act. John of the Cross considers such sensual experience as merely "impure and rebellious acts . . . sensual rebellions, movements, and acts in the senses . . ." which appear frequently and involuntarily "in one's very spiritual exercises . . . when the spirit is deep in prayer or when receiving the sacrament of penance or of the Eucharist . . ."[36] and which will disappear at the most advanced spiritual levels (presumably after the heat of youth is over!). Because of the celibate origins of our spirituality, there is no Christian tradition of approaching God through the medium of sexuality.

· But there has always been an alternative possibility within Christian tradition, epitomized by Maximus the Confessor (580-662), who held that "in man the carnal and the spirit are so united that body itself becomes an expression of the spirit."[37] Thomas Merton and Maurice Nédoncelle, among others, follow in his footsteps today. Merton writes of interior contemplation and external activity not as opposed but as two aspects of the same love of God, pointing out that the experimental awareness of the presence of God is "just as truly a created thing as a glass of beer."[38] Maurice Nédoncelle clearly states the position that both our approach to God and God's response to us may be given through the most varied modes of our experience, including those of the senses.[39]

According to theologians of this school, and as long recognized in Eastern religious traditions, God can operate on our body as well as on our minds. In conjugal ecstasy, magnified physical sensation, overcoming the mind, can itself become an instrument of self-transcendence, freeing the self from the ordinary and the everyday. The intensity of sensory and kinesthetic awareness in sexual climax is a catalyst for growth which, if dedicated, becomes a powerful instrument for spiritual transformation.

Just as the mind through long spiritual exercise is said to acquire "spiritual senses" to see, hear, taste, smell, and touch, so in a conjugal spirituality bodies mutually develop a "language" above and beyond the physical senses, faculties of perception and thought that provide a parallel route to God and knowledge of self and the other unobtainable in any other way. Thus, sensual relating for the couple parallels prayer in motive, technique, fruit, and progression, and can be the road to the heights of prayerful experience of God. Orgasm can be the ground for religious ecstasy.

The work of the Jesuit William Johnston shows a clear progression toward recognizing this. He began in *Silent Music* by suggesting that the principles of friendship developed by the medieval abbot Aelred "might well lead to a mysticism of marriage," that the love, faith, meditation and nonpossessive attachment of couples can develop their interior senses, "leading them through those stages that culminate in the kiss of Christ, a situation where Christ is somehow present in their love as the Spirit is present in the love of the Father for the Son."[40] In *The Inner Eye of Love* he further affirms that lovers may be drawn into "a state of deep, unitive silence where thoughts and concepts become unnecessary and even superfluous, yet where the inner eye, the eye of love, penetrates powerfully to the core of the other's being." He judges this similar to "or in certain cases identical with" mystical states of silence.[41] And finally, in *The Mirror Mind* he states unequivocally that a married person can be an advanced mystic.[42]

The conjugal path of proximity and sacrificial, holy-making action can lead to the same end of mystical awareness and union. Since conjugal ecstasy thus begins from within the sensual realm and is fostered by the bodily faculties, the ascetic task for the couple is to increase rather than to diminish awareness and activity, and to dedicate this sexual thought and action to God until such time as the selves are fully opened to the spirit from beyond, which can alone accomplish the perfection of real union.

The physical practice of sexual union recapitulates all aspects of conjugal dialogue. In it every fluctuation of mood and every spiritual stage and state is perceptible. "Sex" is the word most commonly used for this conjugal discipline. Thus "sex," of all the conjugal disciplines, can with its preliminaries stand most adequately as shorthand for the whole of conjugal asceticism. It is always a gauge of existing unity; if integrated, it is a means toward inner liberty and joy, and if perfected, a source of loving knowledge of God. Present from the beginning in fleeting moments of ecstatic communion when doing and knowing are one, "sex" and the unitive state it represents are the culmination of all preceding stages of conjugal development.

The long-term practice of "sex" is, I have heard privately from individual Christian theologians, "the quickest way to God." One of them reported being told by the abbot of a monastery that "you (couples) go directly, whereas we must struggle a roundabout way." And the word "sex," like the word cleaving, is exceptionally appropriate for this purpose from the etymological point of view. Although we think mainly of "sex" as an act of joining, its root, the Latin word *sexus*, comes from the verb *seco* and means to cut (as reflected in "section"), thus to separate or divide (as in "sect"). Etymologically therefore, "sex" points both to the division and to the joining of persons which must be present in the ascetic practice of a successful couple.

But "sex," despite its increased frequency of use in polite company, is still often a conversation-stopper. The Birds avoid using it in the above quotation, speaking instead of "lovemaking." It is, moreover, too nonspecific, referring to a wide variety of phenomena. When used in connection with religion, for example, it has frequently referred to Tantric or Taoist practices not involving responsible relationship. Because of these difficulties, it would be useful when referring to the couple's spiritual practice to be able to find some nonembarrassing, "technical" term for specifically Christian and conjugal discipline.

One possibility, for example, is "swiving" (from the Indo-European root *swei-*, meaning "bend, turn, swivel, sway") — a good, obsolete, Anglo-Saxon word which also has the advantage of matching the other good Anglo-Saxon words "leaving" and "cleaving." (I am indebted to John Cotter for this term. His up-dating of the hymn known as St. Patrick's Breastplate, which begins "God be in my head, and in my understanding," includes the line "God be in my loins, and in my swiving.")[43] If we could adopt the term "swiving," we would perhaps in the future be more empowered to act, think, write, and talk about the details of conjugal discipline. Perhaps then it could be more widely broadcast, for example, that under rabbinic discipline sex was expected every day for the unoccupied, once a week for ass-drivers, etc.! When couples can at last discuss techniques for swiving as easily as monks share ways to pray, they will cease to be hidden contemplatives and become full citizens in the city of God.

## Parallels and Sources in the Tradition

> "I have given them the glory you gave to me, that they may be one as we are one." (Jn. 17:22)

> "Speak in your hearts on your beds." (Ps. 4:4, literal tr., Jerusalem Bible)

It is an ironic fact that it was the east, which teaches that bodily being is in essence illusory, rather than the west, where Christianity affirms the Word made Flesh, that developed yogic exercises to perfect the body as spiritual instrument and tantric ritual to relate sex to spirituality. The observation by Joseph and Lois Bird that there is little in the tradition to support the awareness of God's presence in sexual relationship is unfortunately quite accurate.[44]

There is, however, substantial (albeit scattered and "underground") support for the notion of conjugal union as a road to the divine from historical as well as contemporary religious and theological figures. Theologians sprinkled throughout the centuries have recommended cultivating the act of love, from Zeno of Verona in the 4th century,[45] to Nicholas Oresme in the 14th,[46] Alfonse Liguori in the 18th, and Evdokimov in the 20th.

One of the earliest modern apologists for this position was Alan Watts, who argued that sexual activity is "an aspect of life no whit less holy than prayer or feeding the poor," and that only "prejudice and insensitivity have prevented us from seeing that in any other circumstances (the height of sexual love) would be called mystical ecstasy . . ."[47] And if the unconventional character of Watts' life inclines us to discount his testimony, there is the more cautious but unimpeachable assessment of William Johnston, S.J., who writes that "the human love union (which he describes as "a God-like temporary fusion of minds and bodies") is similar to (and perhaps in certain cases identical with) the mystical loving silence about which the medievals write."[48]

This thesis is also accepted by some of other religious backgrounds. From the Eastern Orthodox tradition, Soloviev calls sexual loving a chemical theosis, a means for the spiritualization and divinization of the body,[49] and Paul Evdokimov calls it a theophany in which the partners in union become the image of the Trinitarian God.[50] (Others link the couple and the Trinity as well. Anselm, for example, spoke of the vowed human relation as a figure of the Trinity, and D. S. Bailey, in the 20th century, called it "the best finite exemplification of [that Trinitarian] union without confusion or loss of distinction."[51])

Sexual ecstasy as spiritual discipline is defined as sacramental by some, a theophany by others. Watts finds it an adoration of the divine within another[52]; Holmes, Bailey, and Nelson describe it as a door onto the unconditional and a means of communion with God comparable to baptism and the eucharist,[53] for Charles Gallagher, it is Trinitarian intimacy, and a counterpart to prayer. Evola asserts that it is transformative because rousing the sexual impulse moves the deepest layers of our being, its peak a sacred fission of being, reunifying the sexually divided human.[54] Greeley calls it revelation, and Gallagher a counterpart to prayer, both a symbol and a cause of union with God, making spouses holy by drawing them into the inner, Trinitarian life of God.[55] Whether as union or as communion, sexual orgasm is considered by these writers and theologians to be the potential equivalent of mystical ecstasy.

For joint accession to God, couples have a model in the experience of Augustine and his mother, Monica. As for models of union with God, many can be found in the mystical literature of all religious traditions. Sexuality is so closely linked to spirituality that even those who do not cultivate it, experience it. Mystics often are disturbed by the bodily effects of spiritual concentration (cf. John of the Cross above), and it has long been a subject of wonder that mystical literature is more effectively erotic than most of what secular writers can produce. The most well-known example is perhaps Teresa's vision of the cherub who plunged his spear into her heart. Teresa writes of "an angel in bodily form" who "left me completely afire with a great love for God. The pain was so sharp that it made me utter several moans; and so excessive was the sweetness caused me by this intense pain that one can never wish to lose it . . ."[56]

For Biblical models of the mystical goal, swivers can turn to the lifelong love which puts death to flight in the book of *Tobit* and to the original "mystical marriage," the *Song of Songs*, with its erotic description of a loving relationship and its many verses of ecstatic mutuality: "My Beloved is mine and I am his" (2:16); "He is altogether lovable. Such is my Beloved, such is my friend" (5:16); "My dove is unique, mine, unique and perfect" (6:9). Called by Rabbi Akiba the "holy of holies" of scripture,[57] the *Song of Songs* has in the past been allegorized as the story of God's love of Israel. William Johnston, however, writes that the "union (of biological and romantic love) is found clearly in *The Song of Songs*"[58]; and according to Phyllis Trible and other recent writers, this monument to eros tells not of divine-human love itself, at least not directly, but of human love as God's plan of redemption for creation ("I am my Beloved's, and his desire is for me." 7:11) which had at the beginning gone awry ("Your yearning shall be for your husband, yet he will lord it over you" Gen. 3:16).[59] Its conclusion gives lovers an exhortation and a promise: "Set me like a seal on your heart . . . For love is strong as Death . . . The flash of it is a flash of fire . . . Love no flood can quench" (8:6-7).

If the archetypal swivers' book is the *Song of Songs*, their archetypal feast is the feast of Tabernacles, the festival of rest at the climax of the agricultural year, a vacation celebrated in tents or booths or shelters or huts. "When you have harvested the produce of the land, you are to celebrate the feast of Yahweh for seven days. On the first and eighth days there shall be a complete rest. On the first day you shall take choice fruits, palm branches, boughs of leafy trees and willows from the river bank, and for seven days you shall rejoice in the presence of Yahweh your God . . . For seven days you are to live in shelters: all natives of Israel must live in shelters, so that your descendants may know that I made the sons of Israel live in shelters when I brought them out of the land of Egypt. I am Yahweh your God" (Lev. 24:39-43).

The feast of Tabernacles recalled to the Jews the abiding presence of Yahweh during the exodus, the Ark and its cherubim, the conquest of the land (Neh. 8:13-18), the ingathering of fruit (Deut. 16:13-15) and the completion of the temple (I Kg. 8), all themes which can be associated with a conjugal spirituality. In Christian scripture, the feast of Tabernacles came to Peter's mind when Moses and Elijah appeared with Jesus on the mountain of the Transfiguration (Mt. 17:4), and the gospel of John uses it as the setting for Jesus' promise of the Holy Spirit (7:37-40). It is in the celebratory spirit of Tabernacles that Christian couples today can in their own way follow the command of Christ to be one.

# 6

# Conjugal Exercise and Ritual

*"Pleasures are shafts of the glory as it strikes our sensibility . . . Make them channels of adoration."* (C.S. Lewis)

*"Sex is an act of virtue oriented toward growth in mutual sanctity, a spiritual encounter whose ultimate goal is the discovery of the presence of God."* (Caroline Spurgeon)

## The Dyadic Way

THROUGH THE DISCIPLINE OF RADICAL PROXIMITY, the couple dedicates the "one-flesh" as its point of contact with God. Revolving on the axis of their relationship, they enter eternity by exchanges of coinherent love, by intercourse on all levels of consciousness. To grasp the essence of conjugal discipline, it is necessary to shift one's perspective from that of a mind concentrated on a religious subject to that of mind and senses riveted on religious action, from sense as distraction to sense as vehicle and pointer.

Conjugal discipline is shaped by the peculiar nature of the couple, two bodies and minds by their orientation creating one spiritual space. Couples may adapt and adopt all the rules and riches of the celibate tradition for their individual and communal spiritual practice, but their primary focus as couple must be on each other and on the relationship, their primary discipline as couple that of exercise centered in the body. The bodily exercises of conjugal discipline gather together and center "that whole human reality which some people are beginning to call bodymind."[1] This conjugal discipline presupposes that the groundwork has been laid or is being laid in three areas necessary to dyadic discipline. The first is the adequate preparation of each individual as a dedicated offering; the second, a certain expertise in communication and sexual relating, in active listening and empathy, confronting and diplomacy, and in the education of the senses; and finally, real acquiescence to the equal value of both individuals and real recognition and respect of their radical difference. Discipline for the couple, Paul and the tradition notwithstanding, must be based on what Soloviev calls *amor aequalis*, on a love that is not that of superior to inferior, nor that of inferior to superior (i.e., not a reflection of divine/human love), but that of equal to equal (i.e., more like love within the Trinity), no holds barred.

Satisfactory spiritual direction for the couple is difficult to find. Some have stumbled on individuals who were helpful as guides; many have gotten help from support groups which encourage by example and interchange of ideas. But as we have seen in examining the human phenomenon, the couple reveals itself with difficulty. In Eastern Orthodox tradition, direction is theoretically impossible, the marital relation so sacred that no third person can trespass upon it.

There remains, however, the possibility of mutual guidance, a solution proposed by many. Roman Catholic documents have spoken of "mutual inward molding," Methodists, of formation by the covenant relation, and Quakers, of working toward holiness through mutual admonition. Though critics reject the idea of the couple as mutual guides because they find the requisite objectivity is lacking, advocates argue that permanent partners are in the best position to share what is violating the other and to search out the gifts the other can best develop, to provide that "homely dalliance and consoling intercourse" which for Margery Kempe, at least, constituted spiritual direction. Perhaps the best way of thinking about the subject is to say not that the individuals in the couple are each other's spiritual guides, but that the way of radical proximity itself, followed faithfully to the end, provides (not without help from time to time) the spiritual guidance a couple needs, each drawing the other out and being drawn out by attraction into transcendence.

## Exercises of the Chalice

*"The nature of created things is the word of God."*
*(Antony)*

*"One-flesh is divinizing knowledge, becoming perfectly transparent mirrors." (Dionysius Areopagite)*

Benedict taught his monks to think of the monastery's property as a holy chalice. So must couples continue to develop individually in order to give solidity to the profiles which form the shape of the holy space between them. The development of self entails work on personal skills and any remedial physical or psychological exercises necessary, and also includes sexual calisthenics which prepare for meeting the other: gluteal exercise, pelvic tilt, seat lift, hip swing, circle tilts, leg lifts, head to instep exercise, crotch stretch. Women should particularly pay attention to the exercises which tone pelvic muscles. A good presentation of them (as well as an awe-filled introduction to male and female genital geography) is found in Sheila Kitzinger's book.[2]

Equal attention should be given to the "space between" itself, the birthplace of relationship. The two pour their lives into this chalice and give it shape through verbal and no-verbal exchange. This natural process seems easy in the early stages, but may become more difficult as obstacles are experienced and as images harden. Colloquy must nevertheless continue throughout the length of the relationship, uncovering ever more of the past, ever-deeper layers of the present, and ever-changing hopes for the future.

The following is a small, illustrative sample of the endless serious and lighthearted ways couples can carry out that *devoir de s'asseoir*, Marriage Encounter's "ten and ten."

For mutual self-disclosure:

1. Take turns discussing oneself for an agreed period of time (10 minutes?) while the other takes notes; talk about the notes three days later (not to blur personal boundaries).

2. Brainstorm for 10 minutes what plant, color, or animal fits yourself and the other.

3. Try two minutes of gibberish and/or mime to express whatever feelings are current.

To experience and give more shape to the space between:

1. Choose which partner will go first. Beginning 20 feet apart, each in turn, palms out, advances to the distance which makes the "space between" most solid. Eyes on toes, note the space between. Relax, focus a minute on the other, noting boundaries. Advance and retreat slowly to find how far the comfort zone extends.

2. Take five minutes each being the other's shadow, synchronizing movements, as you move to music (Pachelbel's "Canon"? hard rock?).

And to build up the temple, increasing its solidity:

1. Daily confide your individual joys, large or small, rejoicing in the other's. This exchange of gifts is most naturally done at the end of the day, and serves not only to extend pleasure but to increase it through hearing its effect.

2. Jointly determine what creation demands of a durable relation by developing a weekly or monthly wish list. This can be things that need working on, positive or negative, and is best written and exchanged. (Marriage Encounter pioneered the writing of "letters" for couple communication. Writing has since been given many other applications. It has been discovered to be useful for quarreling when it is inexpedient to be overheard, for example!)

3. Develop a private body and sex vocabulary, trying out words for body parts *and actions* that will be your own secret language. What words from the past occur? Those from the 50s may remember that couples did not "go all the way" but "scrounched" on the sofa or in drive-in movies. Keep adding to the list. Share these words with the other and experiment with them in lovemaking. Change them as often as you discover they are unpleasant or worn out. There are always new ones.

If you run out of four-letter words in this last exercise, you might seek out some of the foreign terminologies. (See the bilbliography for source material.) Each part of the body is given a poetic name in many Eastern traditions (the body has nine gates, for example: two lower [the orifices of the anus and the sexual organ] and seven upper [the mouth, nose, eyes, ears and fontanel opening at the top of the head]). In China, since the body is sacred as a temple of the spirit, the names of its parts are preceded by the honorific adjective "jade," or "golden," as the most precious of stones and metals. The base of the skull, for example, is the Jade Pillow, and the feet are the Golden Lotus. Of all parts, the sexual parts are the most sacred. The penis is the Jade Stalk, the vulva, the Jade Gate, and the clitoris, the Jade Peak.

Hindu tradition also has an extensive sexual vocabulary and uses poetic language where we might use scientific terminology. Vaginas are designated according to their depth, from Lute String (one inch) to Inner Door, or North Pole (eight inches). Male sex organs are similarly classified into three types — small, "the hare" (up to six finger-breadths, about five inches); middle, "the bull," to nine finger-breadths (about seven inches); and large, "the horse," about twelve finger-breadths (about ten inches). The Jewel and the Lotus, the Scepter and the Bell, the Wand and the Cup are three of the most familiar visual representations for the male and female sex organs, but Douglas and Slinger list many more, including Jade Stalk and Jade Gate, Crimson Bird and Purple Chamber, Yang Pagoda and Secret Cabinet. There are equally colorful names for kisses (Contact of the Upper Gates), all kinds of positions (Two Fishes Side by Side, Silkworm Spinning a Cocoon) and types of thrust (Seagull Playing on the Waves, Boat Braving the Gale). All human sexual actions and interactions are thus dignified and ennobled by suitably respectful and beautiful designations.

## Exercises of the Ellipse

*"Love thy wife studiously. Gladden her heart all thy life long." (Ancient Egypt)*

*"God is mysteriously present in each exchange of true love between two human persons." (Emery)*

The ellipse can be seen as the sacred oval formed by two inter-linked lives, the place where "conjugal body" exists, and from which conjugal body may explicitly link with God, Christ, and the Trinity. This area of intersection alternately grows and shrinks of itself as the individuals become closer or distance themselves in service or self-development. But considered from the point of view of conjugal discipline, the oval is formed also from within, as the two change and adapt to change within the couple. Exercises of the ellipse, therefore, are of two kinds, those of balance and equilibrium (which are required by the fact that two beings are involved), and those of stretching and synchrony (which are necessary to construct the ellipse -around those two separate points). The first have to do with encounter, therefore with fun and with fighting; the second with wisdom, therefore the ability to extend selves and to be flexible.

A good fight-fair manual should be on every bedtable, so that relationship can become what the philosopher James Carse has described as an "infinite game,"[3] one which is played not to win but simply to continue to play. Since the purpose of the infinite game is to keep both players in play, the rules change whenever the players agree that victory and defeat threaten. Rules in the conjugal life, as in the infinite game, are more like the grammar of a living language than the rules of debate. We observe them as a way of continuing to talk to each other, not as a way of bringing the other person's speech to an end.

For synchrony and a beginner's experience of the Holy Spirit as breath flowing in and out (as in the traditional discipline) and between (as in the conjugal version), a good exercise is skin-to-skin spooning:

1. Arrange for uninterrupted time. Prepare the room for comfort.

2. Decide who will be inside, and spend 10 minutes lying naked back to front, observing each other's respiration and one's

own. At later times, take turns matching the other's rate of breathing.

3. Notice the feeling within the body at the end of the time.

For stretching our knowledge of the other and our skills to please, there are two ways: mapping, to search out the secrets of the body personally, and research, to learn what others have discovered. For research, consult the relevant sections of the bibliography and the shelves of local libraries, bookstores, and video shops.

For mapping:

1. Prepare the room as the garden of Eden, the couple comfortably nude or specially clothed to welcome the mystery of touch, one person on a large beach towel or soft body-sized mat.

2. The other "sees" the body of the first by light touch all over. The person lying down visualizes the body thus revered by the touching hands.

3. The second person experiments systematically for 20 minutes with different kinds of touch on all parts of the first person's body, slow/fast, hard/soft, nails/arms/hair, etc. The first person gives continual, systematic feedback about what is being revealed: sensations pleasant, painful, ecstatic, not so good, etc.

4. At later stages, the first person can experiment with the other non-visual senses, listening to chest, belly, back; smelling hair and pubic hair, hands and armpits; tasting toes, legs, lips.

5. The second person takes the first person's place, and the exercise is repeated.

For exercising the conjugal body in intimacy, there is the pushing-hands exercise, adapted from one used at the Anchorhold in England.[4] There are two basic movements in which each can contact the core energy of the other and experience the enlarging of the oval inhabited by the divine presence. As in the Chinese comprehension of the universe as the interplay of two forces, Yin and Yang, movements are active, pressing or pushing, and passive, rolling back or receiving:

1. Begin with both gently pressing palms against each other.

2. Move slightly to one side or the other, upward or downward, back and forth, each time recentering, feeling the balance and off-balance.

3. One or the other ends the pressing with a gentle push.

4. The two begin playfully pushing and giving way. One ends the session by receiving the forward movement in the arms rather than rolling back.

## Exercises of the Kiss

*"Holy Spirit is like breath exchanged in conjugal kiss."*
*(Fulgence de Ruspe, 5th century)*

*"Sexual union is a fusion in which one discovers God."*
*(Nachmanides)*

Brancusi's "Kiss" is a plastic representation of "Oneing," the experience of bliss, ecstasy, and union. It is not only the brief moment of orgasm, which is the entry into the noneveryday world, but also the door to the feast, the outward harmony that radiates in the sight of others. In the exercises of the kiss, two humans join as one temple of the Spirit and draw on the universal nourishing forces of sensual energy. All empathic power depends on allowing these temporary fusions.[5]

Whether the peak experience is kataphatic, the mind full of the presence of the other, or apophatic, mind carried beyond itself by intensity of sensory and kinesthetic awareness, the other's uniqueness becomes absolute. The other-with-oneself becomes icon, a living vessel of the holy presence, not a means to an end but part of it. This union of persons points to that within the divine unity which theologians call perichoresis.

The Proximate Preparation for exercise of the Kiss is to live as much as possible in unity, setting aside some minutes each day for pleasing the other, sheltering the flame within which fuels the cyclical currents of mutual affection. The Immediate Preparation is to become aware of the "one-flesh," laying other tasks aside, sharing feelings, confessing and offering reassurance if love has recently been neglected, clothing or unclothing to honor the body.

To begin:

1. Jointly choose words of entry into the Presence for opening the session.

2. Prepare the selves and the setting; build a festival booth with "willow branches and choice fruit."

3. Facing each other, recite the invocation you have chosen.

4. Concentrate in stillness and silence, looking into the other's eyes. Chain the demons of dailiness, focus the entire attention on the God-force within and the other's infinite value.

5. Slowly circumambulate, one by one, as in the exercises of the chalice.

6. Center yourselves and rest again in each other's presence. Remind yourself that sex is never absent, only our awareness of it.

7. Approaching within touch-distance, be aware of the breath's passage from each into the space between. Center your meditation on the connection of hearts through the breath.

8. Close with each other. Meditate using the five senses. Experience the circuit of energy circling slowly through the joined bodies.

9. Honor each other's body in the ways you have discovered in the exercises of the ellipse, for the length of time which seems good to both, repeating the invocation, or the other's name.

10. Rest and reflect on the fire in heart.

## Ritual

The couple, as was seen in the first chapter, does not have depth of history in its forms for prayer and patterns for living. These are just beginning to evolve out of accumulating experience as couples become conscious of their vocation and practice it. More rites and rituals are needed, at least one for recognizing the spiritual birth (and rebirth) of the couple as "one-flesh," and one to nourish the conjugal soul in its life.

The "monk not manqué" who married after trying out as a Trappist spoke of the commitment undertaken at his wedding as his "simple vow" (the provisional vows from which monastics can be without further ado dispensed), and the birth of his first child as the "solemn," or permanent, irrevocable ones.[6] From a conjugal perspective, it would be useful for the "simple vows" of the wedding ceremony always to be supplemented after a period of time by "solemn" ones confirming the intent of permanence, and sometimes by a further form of celebration to mark the time when the couple fully realizes the spiritual potential of their coupledom and becomes ready to assume it as the religious vocation which the church defines it to be.

There is evidence of the existence of such a rite in the "sacrament of the bridal chamber" mentioned in early Christian texts. One such is The Gospel of Philip,[7] a "gnostic" Christian text written probably between 250 and 300 A.D., that is to say, within the relatively early period when Jewish conjugal traditions would still have been at home in Christianity. The material in the text is fragmentary, and the Valentinian worldview it contains so radically different from ours that experts are not yet agreed on how it views sexuality, but it could well be interpreted as evidence of a Christian environment geared toward conjugal holiness and a ritual expression growing out of conjugal experience.

In the theology of these Valentinians, it was the division of the sexes, not disobedience of divine command (as in Genesis), which was at the root of the human problem. Christ came to earth to redeem humanity by providing a means of reunification, the sacrament of the bridal chamber, in which an experience of the original Edenic androgyny is transmitted. This rite was particularly important because entrance into the Christian community was not, as later became the case, through baptism but through "chrism," or anointing, which was given in the rite of the bridal chamber. ("The chrism is superior to baptism, for it is from the word 'chrism' that we have been called 'Christians,' certainly not because of the word 'baptism.' And it is because of the chrism that 'the Christ' has his name . . . He who has been anointed possesses everything. He possesses the resurrection, the light, the cross, the Holy Spirit. The Father gave him this in the bridal chamber . . .".[8]) The text compares the "bridal chamber" to that most sacred place of the Jews, the innermost part of the temple, into which only the high priest entered, and that only once a year ("Baptism is the Holy building . . . The Holy of the Holies is the bridal chamber"[9]). With the death of Christ "the veil was rent . . . the holies of the holies were revealed, and the bridal chamber invited us in."[10]

The details of this rite and its relevance to individuals rather than to couples (perhaps in this Jewish/Christian context only couples were initiated?) remain maddeningly unavailable to us. There are only tantalizing snippets, such as the statement that the participants received, probably through anointing, "a male power or a female power — the bridegroom and the bride," in the rite of "the mirrored bridal chamber"[11] ("As above, so below"?) Barring the discovery of further texts, our curiosity will doubtless remain unsatisfied. The sacrament of the bridal chamber in some groups apparently included actual sexual intercourse for those receiving the sacrament. Clement of Alexandria, writing disapprovingly that they believed it would "bring them to God,"[12] accepted only the Valentinian "gnostics" whose use of intercourse, according to his information, was exclusively symbolic.

We know from other sources that other communities were also making connections between the sexual and the spiritual. We hear charges (from their opponents) that 2nd-century "Alphites" practiced sexual affection and bodily contact, that the 4th-century bishop Priscillian prayed "stark naked," "holding nightly meetings with immoral women,"[13] and that both Kabbalistic Jews and Gnostic Christians, who were called Ophites, practiced (metaphorically? actually?) a scandalous ritual communion in which a couple offered up the "living substance of reproduction" rather than "dead" bread and wine representing "the dead body of God."

Were these "nightly meetings" indeed simple orgies "with immodest women" as charged by their detractors? Were the 2nd and 3rd century "Adamites" in north Africa indeed promiscuous, as accused by Augustine and Epiphanius? And was the bridal chamber too, as some charge, simply a pagan rite ("pastos," the inner temple chamber) in which male initiates mated with the representative of the

Goddess, and female initiates with the representative of her divine consort? Or did *The Gospel of Philip* and at least some of these groups, of which all but the condemnatory fragments have been obliterated, indeed reflect environments oriented toward conjugal growth, with sacramental practices designed to nurture conjugal holiness? Even as it stands, *The Gospel of Philip* is at least testimony to a worldview more congenial to our modern ideals for relationship than the view which ultimately prevailed.

A public rite of actual sexual intercourse is difficult to imagine from the perspective of a modern, still "puritanical," though theoretically liberated society. It is even difficult for some to imagine intercourse as a private rite. Things have not always been exactly as they are now, however. In medieval times, priest and acolyte would accompany couples to the bridal bed and bless them there with candles and incense. Further back, Christians living in a Hellenistic society would certainly not have been as shocked by public nudity as we are today, when even the rabidly liberal city of Berkeley, California, found itself obliged to pass a law against it.

It is possible to wonder whether a positive valuation of sexuality may not eventually lead to some meaningful acknowledgement of it within our own public worship. Looking to the future as a progression toward the Omega Point of which Teilhard de Chardin spoke, the "evolutionary leap" confidently predicted by Soloviev, and the "second axial period" heralded by Ewert Cousins,[14] we can dream that one day conjugal union may be frankly acknowledged, fully honored, and sacramentally celebrated within the bounds of the church building. Two perfectly imaginable beginnings with the weight of tradition behind them, for example, would be to reinstate the lost words "With my body I thee worship" among the conjugal vows and to revalorize the annual plunging of the Paschal candle into the baptismal font at Easter vigil services. (For a vivid presentation of the natural symbolism in this rite, I recommend Derrick's *Sex and Sacredness*.[15])

Until then, we can only regret the lost rituals of earliest Christianity, and look with awe and wonder at the impressive remains of other ancient rites which reflect societies where sexuality was looked on as natural in the way that a naked body is considered unexceptional in the bath or in a nudist colony, and in which the sexual life, being of vital concern to the society, was central to religious life and was given spiritual support and guidance.

Concrete examples of such possibilities do exist. There were as late as the early Christian centuries public Taoist rites which were at one and the same time a social "coming of age" and a sexual initiation. These flourished particularly from 22 to 220 A.D. in parts of China, but like the rite of the bridal chamber, were subject to abuse and therefore to criticism, and were prohibited in 440 A.D. Their influence nevertheless lingered, and one symbolic variety was practiced in China until quite recently.

License for drawing judiciously on such Eastern resources for conjugal practice may perhaps be found in the connection of the wisdom of Solomon with the East and with cults honoring a divine couple. In Solomon's times Israel was known to have commercial contacts with India, and the *Song of Songs* (which is enshrined in the scriptures and is number one of the five great scrolls, the one read each year at Jewish Passover celebrations) is judged by many scholars to be a liturgical fragment from the Canaanite cult of Tammuz and Ishtar.

Moreover, the sex which in the Indian Tantric Yoga tradition is spoken of as *kundalini,* potential energy (literally "coiled snake," connected with the word *kunda,* a basin, bowl, or pool), has been associated by at least one writer with the Christian idea of the Holy Spirit, "a spiritual element in the material." Herbert Slade points out that in St. John's Gospel the water of the Spirit is described as "an inner spring always welling up for eternal life" (Jn. 4:14), and the man filled with the Spirit is told that "Streams of living water shall flow out from within him" (Jn. 7:38).[16] In the Indian myth, when the *kundalini* is aroused, it travels through all the centers of the body and culminates in loving union with God.

In the Taoist *Yellow Book* tradition, as described by Okada, young couples obtained evidence of their worthiness from elders in their community, and prepared themselves for the rite by abstinence and ritual bath. Perfuming themselves with incense, they enter the meditation hall with a reader (required to coach them through the complicated ritual), their character witnesses, and a written copy of their credentials. The secret rite then takes place in 20 stages with great solemnity, the ceremonial entrance, stations to be taken within the hall, ritual actions and words, all minutely prescribed (standing on the left, the male initiate inserts his right index finger between the female initiate's left index and middle fingers) and punctuated by the sounding of a drum.

In the first part of the ceremony, the couple carry out many traditional Taoist visualizations and meditations, accompanied by breathing exercises (a lump between the eyebrows gradually growing in size and brilliance, illuminating their bodies until all organs, bones, muscles, tendons and cavities are visible; the air of the four seasons with their characteristic colors invigorating the body, coursing from the nose to the genitals and back up to the head, three times; the airs of heaven, earth and water likewise). Invoking the gods and goddesses individually, they perform symbolic actions of escaping the dangers which threaten those who approach the sacred; then invoking the deities in pairs, they carry out "enlivening movements" (playing, turning, mingling, wrestling, pushing).

This preparation over, the master undresses the initiates and takes down their hair, the reader taking down the hair of the witnesses to signal the beginning of the part of the rite involving intimate physical contact. The initiates, continuing their breathing exercises, alternately sit and lie with clasped hands; then reciting a passage from scripture, the man lies on top of the woman, first with feet, hips, shoulders, chest, and eyebrows touching, then with his head to the east, the female's to the south. Circumambulations, further visualizations, breathing, and meditations follow, each minutely specified.

Then the man begins a prescribed pattern of erotic stroking, and as the pair recite and chant formulas stating and affirming the meaning of their actions, he penetrates and performs the proper sequence of movements and thrusts, the pair synchronizing their breathing in predetermined patterns (three-five-seven-nine; two-four-six-eight). Withdrawal and further ritual breathing and stroking take place gradually. Both lie on their backs, pass clasped hands over the cranium twelve times, tap their teeth three-five-seven-nine times, swallow their saliva and inhale slowly three-five-seven-nine times. Then, hands crossed over the forehead, each meditates on bringing the airs back into the various organs of the body (spleen, kidneys, lungs, heart), performing one set of rubbing of hands, face and body to warm them, followed by visualization of the air from the nostrils covering the face, and another set followed by visualizing the air moving from the feet up the spine to the head, then down the forehead, front and through the five organs back to the toes, until the air is finally stored in the genitals. With further symbolic actions performed to avoid misfortune and promote fertility, they give thanks and leave, chanting, making a gesture of "breaking away with both hands" as they come out of the door.

Public ceremonies of this kind are, of course, unthinkable in our society, though many couples, as Evdokimov recommended, draw on them for private practice. Until such time as communities begin to accept sexual practice as spiritually relevant, recognize the need for some such two-staged entry into conjugal life as exists in monastic vocation, and devise suitable rites to accommodate it, the only options available to couples wishing to acknowledge a deepened awareness of the spirit in their lives are a reaffirmation of vows, as is used in Marriage Encounter weekends, or some individually created ceremony. One could be developed from what we can gather about those early, lost rites or more traditional rites such as the following.

## Hand-fasting

Over a preparatory period of time, the couple each prepare, separately and jointly, and perhaps in consultation with a "soul-friend," a statement setting forth their understanding of the spiritual significance of their life together and the specifics of the commitment which they wish to formalize. Having prepared an appropriate place and invited a few friends to be their witnesses, they gather at the appointed time and read the statements they have composed. Joining hands (right hands, both hands, or both hands crossed), they make their vows to each other, and conclude by reciting or singing with their witnesses a suitable celebratory passage or hymn (such as the following verses taken from *The Song of Songs*) in order to connect with the tradition. After this, the assembled company may join hands with the couple, singing other songs or enjoying a circle-dance:

Witnesses: Awake, O north wind, and come, O south wind!

O you who dwell in the gardens, my companions are listening for your voices; let us hear them.

1: Behold, you are beautiful, my love; behold, you are beautiful.

2: Draw me after you, let us make haste.

1: Set me as a seal upon your heart,

2: For love is strong as death.

1: Its flashes are flashes of fire, a most vehement flame.

2: Many waters cannot quench love, neither can floods drown it.

1: Arise, my love, my fair one, and come away; for lo, the winter is past, the rain is over and gone.

2: The flowers appear on the earth, the time of singing has come, and the voice of the turtledove is heard in our land.

1: The fig tree puts forth its figs, and the vines are in blossom; they give forth fragrance.

2: Arise, my love, my fair one, and come away.

1: Make haste, my beloved, and be like a gazelle,

2: Or a young stag upon the mountains of spices.

Together: I am my beloved's and my beloved is mine.

Witnesses: Eat, O friends and drink: drink deeply, O lovers!

We will exult and rejoice in you; we will extol your love more than wine.

In addition to a ceremony of institution, the couple also needs one which would be for them (as the eucharist is for the ecclesiastical body of Christ) a weekly replenishing of spiritual energy, a continuing source of nourishment to supplement their everyday conjugal prayer. For this, couples can draw both on the Eastern rites above and the conjugal traditions of Judaism which influenced early Christianity. We know, for example, that from the earliest times, even after their expulsion from the synagogues, Jewish Christians continued the customs of their Hebrew forbears, becoming couples in a ceremony called *qiddusin*, or "sanctification," with fasting, confession, contract, blessings, robes, crowns, veil, procession and feast. As late as the end of the 4th century, John of Chrysostom still mentions "seven days of feasting, as in Judaism."[17] Attendance at this *qiddusin* was as obligatory as observing the major yearly feasts for the Jews.[18] It conferred divine significance on the human relationship, including its physical pleasures.

The *qiddusin* and its ritual renewal by sexual intercourse on the sabbath vigil or on the sabbath (the time of joy and rest) signified the union of heaven and earth, of God and his Shekinah (i.e., Glory), or later, for Christians, of Christ and the Church. As Mohler notes, "The prayer habits of the early Christians followed those of the synagogue."[19]

We also know that Christians began early to change Jewish practice to reflect Christian teaching. *The Apostolic Tradition*, a compact bishop's manual written about 200 A.D., echoes Hebrew custom in recommending that Christians pray seven times a day, the last time rising from bed at midnight to join creation in greeting and praising Christ the Bridegroom.[20] But the manual goes on to specify that sexual union is not (as for the Jews) a ritual impediment making the partners "unclean." It is explicitly stated that Christians who have had intercourse during the evening do not have to wash themselves in order to become ritually "pure," but simply to sign themselves with their "moist breath" (perhaps thereby to make the symbolic gesture more personal) and "so" to spread "spittle" on their bodies with their hand.[21] If, as some suggest, the word translated "spittle" is not spittle but semen, the text is even more clearly aimed at developing a Christian version of the Jewish ritual sense for intercourse, the sexual union celebrated as an eschatological sign of God's kingdom where all will be one.

Thus the couple may develop a practice of their own by drawing on the Eastern rites, by further exploring the conjugal traditions of Judaism, or by fitting some skeleton such as the following to their own specific situation.

## Con-templ-ation

1. Arrange the room as a fitting setting: bed, pillows, closed curtains, chosen religious symbol.

2. Prepare the body: adorn, clothe/unclothe, wash, oil, massage, stretch, dance.

3. Sit facing each other. Get comfortable: feet parallel, relax head, ears, nose, mouth, neck, heart, belly, and base.

4. Recite a chosen phrase, such as: "Hope deferred makes the heart sick, desire fulfilled is a tree of life" (Prov. 13:12). Simultaneously salute the body of the other (the unveiled Tree of Life) and the God-force within it (hands over head, bend slowly to touch the floor; or bow, palms together at the heart, fingers pointing upward); or taking turns, acknowledge that "You are a member of Christ's body, a little lower than the angels," or honor each other with pillow, shawl, or foot massage.

5. Focus a few minutes on the breath as a sign of the Spirit's activity within yourself, in the space between, and in the other. Share singing (a single note, a repeated phrase, or a longer sequence) to synchronize the breath.

6. Let the other pass out of sight as you take turns moving one at a time around the other, always facing the same direction, focusing on the connected breath and hearts.

7. Move toward the other with outstretched arms, giving and receiving the kiss of peace.

8. Repeat name or "I love you" as a mantra while alternating caresses with awareness of reaction within and reaction of other. Through attentive movements of pressing, pushing, and receiving, mentally and physically experience the energy and inner spirit of the other and join together in the divine presence.

9. Afterward, rest for a considerable period for recollection of the rainbow. Rejoice in the connection, radiate the love outward.

Such sacramental celebrations, traditional or personal, can in effect serve to constitute the two celebrants as "cherubim" and to recognize their offered lives as a cultic sacrifice, a vehicle for the working of divine forces and the awareness of God's presence as Lover. By ritual entrance into intentionality, couples can transcend their secular being and assume triunal, archetypal identities as Lover, Beloved, and Love.

# 7

# Implications

*"Beloved, let us love one another; for love is of God, and he who loves is born of God and knows God. He who does not love does not know God; for God is love"* *(I Jn. 4:7-8)*

*"[They] saw him [dwelling] in the Monad and in the Dyad [and] in the Tetrad." (Valentinian Exposition)*

I HAVE FOCUSED PRIMARILY ON THE LONG-TERM COUPLE as the specialists in conjugal spirituality, the clearest model for the unseparated, unsilent, and unsolitary. I have scoured Christian and non-Christian sources to reconstruct, justify, explain, and support that couple as a spiritually significant entity. I have discovered that spiritually the ideal couple are friends who become through adoption "one-flesh" kin, and start on the high-wire act of prolonged equilibrium and harmony, transcending self, background, suffering, and duality of being, moving with ever-changing intensity toward the glimpsed revelation, the reality of trinitarian union. As they succeed, as deity invades duality to make one and three, they are progressively transfigured, giving to themselves and others a glimpse of the kingdom to come. Through communion, interpenetration, indwelling, and coinherence, their comfortable oneness shows forth the presence of Christ.

I have also discovered that the couple on earth sometimes approaches that ideal, like Prometheus stealing divine fire for humans, but more often it is like Sisyphus, rolling a stone forever upward, only to have it tumble down just before reaching the peak. To form the closest imaginable community, the couple needs faith to choose each other and change and choose each other again, faith in their latent genius for sanctity and in God's power to work through fleshly as well as through mental faculties.

The couple as specialist, ideal or real, cannot pretend to be the archetype of all relation. Christianity's abandonment of the sacramental "bridal chamber" as initiatory rite makes it clear that in the Christian tradition, each person is fully human without being joined to another. Nevertheless the couple as the most intense form of equal one-to-one relatedness has much to contribute to single and communal practice. One-to-one relationship is of importance in all spiritual development. Loving relationship of itself produces antibodies against egotism and provides a training ground for creating wider and wider circles of love.

## Single Cultivation

*"The law of love is the deepest law of our nature . . . Every event of life on earth plants something in the soul." (Merton)*

*"The individual does not exist apart from interaction." (Sullivan)*

The couple's experience is relevant to the individual because whenever contact occurs, conjugal being comes into existence. In the broad sense, all beings and all relations are con-jugal, literally yoking or joining with. All should look for the presence and action of God in relationships and in their impact, pay attention to encounter and interpenetration, and to the newness within which these conjugal realities cause. In the words of one of our earliest theologians, "Where two, there also is the Holy One."[1] If the gnostics were right, division is at the root of the human problem, and the solution for the human problem is reconciliation and reunification. The unpartnered as well as the partnered must cultivate conjugal discipline, mastering the sexual dimension of life, learning to give of self to create relationship without losing personal integrity, to know others without using "the force that kills love."

God is present "in between" and "for" pairing as in between and for the couple. The unpartnered, too, though they do not embody total commitment, become cherubim in relation and create new space for God. The criteria for evaluating disciplines — habitual attentiveness to the other and the education of the senses — are for them the same. The stages or aspects of conjugal spirituality are likewise the same — the revelatory "glimpse," the holy interlinking of lives, and the unitive experience.

## Adoration as Creation

*"The main principle is that action must be accompanied by nondualism between 'head' and 'heart.'"*
*(Advayasiddhe)*

*"Visible creatures are theophanies of God."*
*(John Scotus Erigena)*

Conjugal spirituality for the individual begins (like dual cultivation for the couple) with renunciation and the "good work" of creating relationship, though in this case multiple ones and in different forms. Renunciation is an inevitable part of choosing one over another, and self-transcendence is frequently called for to establish and sustain dialogue in daily relations. Attracted by some degree of the divine spark showing forth from within another person, by the recognition of value that initiates what we call liking and love, individuals are drawn out of themselves toward others, and enter into dialogue which, if continued, progressively creates unseen strands of bonding. Individuals, like couples, will be judged on Judgment Day by what they have experienced of pleasurable encounter.

The holy chalice of colloquy forms as two begin to know each other, using the general conjugal discipline of seeing the world from the other's point of view, while keeping their own identity and objectivity. Individuals can adapt the exercises in the last chapter to cultivate awareness of this "space between" and dedicate it as *templum*. For example, individuals can make the effort to cultivate mutual self-disclosure with a friend. They can also consciously, at least once a day, take note of the distances between them and the humans around them, contemplate the meaning implied in those spaces, and observe the changes that take place as distances are lengthened or narrowed. Insofar as the individual pays attention to the spiritual dimension which exists in the spaces between themselves and others, their relationships can become instruments for spiritual transformation.

## Cooperation as Transformative

*"Interpenetration of personal being is a fact of human existence." (Baelz)*

*"God is experienced in ordinary actions." (Hooker)*

The ellipses of relationship alternately grow and shrink, some minuscule, others large slices of shared sacred history. Relating to others as whole persons, whether or not the relationship itself is highly developed, leads to individual spiritual growth, giving an opportunity to cultivate the art of the *magnus amor*. Nonpossessive attachment develops spiritual sensitivity and the ability to extend oneself, to be flexible.

The individual, like the couple, can use fight-fair manuals to master communicating, confronting, and diplomacy. The individual also stands to grow from better knowing and pleasing others, and can practice a nonphysical version of "mapping" by active listening and empathy. For fully conjugal practice, the individual should also be mindful of the sexual, and honor the physical dimension involved in each relation.

For these purposes, the exercises of the chalice can be extended and given more concreteness by including, in the attentiveness to the "space between," attentiveness also to the breath flowing in and out of it, as was perceived by touch in the conjugal spooning exercise. Synchronizing and shadowing can also be adapted for the single cultivation of conjugal spirituality. Experts in salesmanship have long noted the effectiveness of subtly copying another person's position, manner, and speech style in creating the sense of trust and of being "in-it-together" that brings the buyer to buy. The comradely shove on the shoulder is a natural variant of the pushing-hands exercise, indicating, increasing, and outwardly expressing the inner harmony which has been achieved.

## Communion and Celebration

*"An instant of pure love is more precious in the eyes of God and more profitable for the Church than all other good works together." (Carthusians, and John of the Cross)*

*"You eternalize whatever you love enough. Christ spent time creating a community. 'Follow me' means 'have a personal relation.'" (Evely)*

Whenever the inner eye intuitively penetrates the core of another, a kind of oneness occurs. When there is mutuality, joy is multiplied. As has been noted, these subtle fusions of personal relation are necessary to empathy, thus to the being and well-being of the social fabric. And as Augustine testified, the temporary annihilation of time and space which allows contact with God can occur in conversation as well as in sexual activity.

The completeness of the "one-soul" union that takes place between the deeply attached is a powerful means of learning the love of God and of going to God. In the unitive single, as in the unitive dual stage, "the more we are present for each other, the more He is present to us." When intimacy is present, any pair verges on becoming a couple, celebrating the "space between," community of being, and ecstasy.

Conjugal spirituality thus has implications for single spirituality, as well as for the long-term dyad. Although that perfect oneness "as the Father and I are one" which Christ invoked for the disciples belongs for singles and couples alike to the Alpha and the Omega, the beginning world of Genesis and end time of Revelation, all spiritual self-examination and guidance should include this expanding, conjugal part of the soul.

## Other Ramifications

*"All being is an imperfect image of God." (Dionysius Areopagite)*

*"I am androgynous." (Trimorphic Protenoia)*

Though a radical proposal, conjugal spirituality clearly reflects current religious and societal developments. Physicians now are being urged to be partners in the patient's health care rather than directors of it. Management is being retrained to become less authoritarian and hierarchical. Spiritual directors are becoming "soul friends."

I have made every effort by accumulating bits and pieces from historical sources to show that this spirituality has its roots firmly within the tradition, but it cannot be denied that a truly conjugal spirituality is a revolutionary one. Its adoption would pose radical problems for institutions as currently constituted. There are three problems in particular which come to mind.

First, it would mean the recognition and acceptance of the traditionally marginalized and stigmatized, the sexually active of all sorts. Second, it would necessitate the admission of the feminine to the Godhead. And third, it would lead to a resurrection of the *hieros gamos*, a "reincarnation" of spiritual marriage.

Because of the extreme explosiveness of these complex and very important issues and because the community does not yet appear to be on the point of finding universally satisfying solutions for them, I have not attempted to address them at all directly. I have thus in describing conjugal spirituality remained as much as possible at the general level, focusing, for example, on relationship rather than marriage, and on the Trinity rather than the Father, the Son, and the Holy Spirit or any of its innumerable alternatives.

Though I admittedly have no answers to these questions, I am convinced that the revisionist spiritual system I am proposing, based on a worldview in which the "spirit is not in the I but between I and You . . . not like the blood that circulates in you but like the air in which you breathe,"[2] will contribute to the finding of those answers. Long ago, Carl Jung predicted that the West would produce its own yoga on the basis laid down by Christianity.[3] I believe conjugal spirituality to be just such a distinctively Western yoga.

# Appendix A

# Married Saints

---

The following is a fair summary of the categories of conjugal life as portrayed in the saints' lives in *The Penguin Dictionary of Saints*, Omar Englebert's *The Lives of Saints*, and *The Oxford Dictionary of Saints:*

1. Marriage unmentioned: One account records that the 5th century theologian, Prosper of Aquitaine, is "suspected" of being married but that the fact is not certain; others avoid the issue. Englebert makes no mention at all of the marriage of Stephen (975-1038), the evangelizer of Hungary, or, more surprisingly, of the two marriages of Thomas More (1478-1535), the "man for all seasons."

2. Martyrs: St. Exuperius, his wife St. Zoe, and their two children, Christian slaves tortured and put to death by their master sometime between 117 and 138, were honored for dying rather than for living. We can have only the dimmest perception of the conjugal unity which undergirded this joint martyrdom, so these early saints can provide at best only metaphorical models for the Christian life, conjugal or celibate.

3. Widows and widowers who donated their wealth and remaining years to the care of the poor or to founding monastic institutions: One such example is Paula (347-404), who founded monasteries in Bethlehem, and spent 20 years studying Scripture, doing manual work, giving alms, practicing severe austerities, and singing psalms in the church six times a day, clearly a "celibate" rather that a conjugal model of sanctity. We are told nothing of her life with her husband up to the age

of 32. The same is true for Maria Victoria Fornari (1562-1617), who had eight happy years of marriage but is remembered for her next 16 as an abbess occupied with prayer and good works; or Alphonsus Rodriguez (1531-1617), the Jesuit laybrother whose wife and two children died young. For these saints, conjugal life is only referred to in passing, and is totally incidental to their subsequent eremitical or monastic vocation.

4. Parents of well-known saints: Here the conjugal life could, by stretching a point, be said to be valued, but it is still peripheral rather than primary, neutral rather than positive. Into this category fall Monica (331-387), the mother of the theologian Augustine; Nonna (4th century, her exact dates are not given), who had three canonized children (Gregory, Caesarius, and Gorgonia), and Macrina the Elder (also 4th century, also without exact dates), remembered for three famous grandchildren (Macrina the Younger, Basil, and Gregory of Nyssa). We are told in the *Penguin Dictionary of Saints* that both of Basil's parents were canonized, but we do not even know their names.

5. Converters of pagan or wayward spouses: Into this category fall Clotilde (ca. 480-545), who converted the 5th century Frankish king Clovis, and Katherine of Genoa (1447-1510), who by her example succeeded in changing her quick-tempered, dissolute, and unfaithful husband, Julian Adorni. In this category, it is not the marriage which is held up for our admiration and imitation, but the spiritual influence and power of the individual.

6. Those who prefer the celibate life to marriage: St. Abraham, for example, fled his wedding festivities to wall himself up for solitary prayer, only leaving his cell twice thereafter, once at the bishop's request to evangelize a pagan village and once to convert a niece from her life of sin. (A more famous and more dramatic 5th-century Roman legend tells the story of Alexis, who left his bride at the altar, being determined to pursue holy poverty in a foreign country. Although he is finally driven by famine back to his father's house, where his betrothed is still faithfully waiting, he is made known only 17 years later when

the pope is led by a celestial voice to discover him in rags, dead under his father's staircase.)

A call to the "religious" life could and can always set aside the vows of marriage. Gregory of Nyssa, for example, lived until midlife with a well-regarded wife, but was persuaded then to leave her and to join his brother and friend in the monastic life, a course of action applauded by the chroniclers. Similarly, Peter Orseolo, the 10th-century doge of Venice, was canonized after leaving his wife and son (abruptly, without a word) at the age of 50 to become a Trappist in the Pyrenees.

7. Those who leave unhappy marriages for the celibate life: More sympathetic than some are Paul the Simple (4th century), who left his unfaithful wife at the age of 60 to join St. Antony in the Egyptian desert, and Gomer, an 8th-century soldier who, having been given as reward for his services (!) a wife of "a frightful disposition," fled to a solitary place in Belgium.

8. Those who abstain from sexual intercourse: The charitable works and six children of Hedwig of Silesia are mentioned in passing, but fulsome detail and acclaim is reserved for her vow of continence, and for the "celibate" virtues of fasting, long hours of prayer, and sleeping on hard ground. Significantly, aside from the martyrs, Basil's nameless parents, and Isidore the Laborer whose wife was venerated for miracles which occurred after the discovery of her skull long after her death, there is only one case in which both husband and wife were canonized, that of Henry II and Cunegund; and this was facilitated by their zealous support of Benedictine monasticism and probably by the posthumous rumor that they had always lived in continence.

9. Those whose marriage is a trial leading to the perfection of one of the spouses: Here at last the relationship itself is spiritually significant, but only as a new variation of the old theme of martyrdom. The model which is no model finally becomes an anti-model. Consider the cautionary tale of Blessed Seraphina Sforza, who was married in 1448 to a widower. Despite her good care of his duchy while he was away at war, he treated her publicly as a servant when he returned, having in the

meantime fallen in love with a doctor's wife. He beat her in public, dragging her by the hair, tried to strangle her once, and to poison her several times, leaving her half-paralyzed. She finally consented to become a Franciscan nun.

Or the 15 years of common life in which Radegunde (518-587) "perfectly fulfilled all her duties," though married by force to the man she regarded as the murderer of her father; or the 42 years of neglect, infidelity, and unjust suspicion endured by Isabel of Portugal (1271-1336), who raised her husband's illegitimate children and was banished to a fortress for a time; or Blessed Anna Maria Taigi (1796-1837), who is praised for spending 47 years as the perfect wife, mother and housekeeper despite being married to a "peevish servant"!

Tales of spousal mistreatment are largely but not exclusively feminine — some husbands suffered as well. Indeed, it is a male, Gengou Gengulphus, who is the patron saint of those unhappily married. He fared even less well than Seraphina. An 8th-century Burgundian nobleman, he was eventually murdered by his "flighty" wife's accomplice.

There are many more colorful examples which could have been included, some with morbidly amusing appeal, but I have confined myself to those still anthologized. Nevertheless, the overall pattern is unmistakable, and holds unchanged even when one looks at the list of saints canonized in the 20th century. Rita of Cascia (1381-1457, cd. 1900), married only in deference to her parents, endured a rough, ill-tempered, profligate husband for nearly 20 years, and became an Augustinian nun who experienced the stigmata of the crown of thorns. Four widow/foundresses were also canonized in the 20th century, as well as Thomas More (1478-1535) and Nicholas von Flue (1417-1487). Von Flue is remembered for his 19 years as a hermit rather than 18 as husband and father of 10 children.

The case of Thomas More is particularly interesting because it has been considered an exception to the rule by some. Selden Delany, early in the century, interrupted work on a book entitled *Married Saints* because he had come to the conclusion that the Church was inclined to regard sanctity as impossible outside the "religious" life, and that saints were not canonized until their spouses were dead. He was so reassured, however, by Thomas More's canonization that he finally agreed to publish his book in 1935. Here at last, he thought, was a married saint.

But was he? More's beloved wife died young, and when he quickly remarried, it was to a widow (other accounts of her are not flattering) who could mother his young children. His household was heavily Benedictine in style. Donald Attwater can speak only of the "integrity of his God-centered life," meaning his Christian humanism; and Englebert writes of him without mentioning that he was married at all. More's life was not strikingly conjugal in character, to say the least.

Among the latest saints to be beatified are two Italian girls who died resisting rape, a young French victim of the Nazis who never got the chance to marry, a lifelong bachelor physician from Naples, and a 17th-century Philippine husband who left wife and children to go to Japan with a group of missionaries, all canonized by John Paul II. In 1993, he also canonized Maurizio Tornay, a Swiss missionary killed in an ambush in Tibet (1949); Florida Cevoli (18th-century) a Tuscan nun; Joanna Gabriel, the Polish-born nun (d. 1926) who founded a house for novitiates in Rome; and Marie-Louise Trichet, a French nun (born in 1684) who helped found the Daughters of Wisdom, an order that runs schools and hospitals on five continents.

In all fairness, however, I must admit that the anthologies do take note of some happy marriages lasting over a respectable period of time. There were, over the 2,000 years covered, exactly six. The following is a fair summary of the specifically conjugal detail given about the saints in these "good marriages": 1) Matilda (c. 895-968), queen in Westphalia, "lived for more than 20 years in perfect amity" with her husband. 2) Ida (1040-1113), countess of Boulogne, was "always on good terms" with her husband. 3) Hedwig (1174-1243) and her husband "lived in perfect union. Only two disagreements [disagreements fully narrated, by the way!] are recorded in 52 years." Her husband was "a man of religious disposition who helped and encouraged his wife's numerous charitable enterprises." 4) Bridget (c. 1303-1373) went on pilgrimage with her husband, who, becoming ill on the homeward journey, "placed on his wife's finger a gold ring which he asked her to keep as a token of their mutual and undying love." 5) Frances of Rome (1384-1440) had a husband who returned broken from political exile; she cared for him from 1414 to 1436 when he died "after a married life of 40 years without a quarrel." 6) Blessed Amadeus of Savoy (1435-1472), "attacked by epilepsy, actually shared his power with his wife, the duchess. Nevertheless [!] the union of the two remained unbroken . . ."

From these examples we gather that conjugal sanctity might consist in perfect amity (Matilda, Ida, and Frances of Rome), mutual and undying love (Bridget), and perfect union (Hedwig and Amadeus of Savoy), which might be fostered by the equality of the persons involved (Amadeus). But of the spiritual means of reaching this ideal we learn nothing. We could only conclude, possibly, that a common religious disposition (Hedwig and Bridget) is an advantage. In each of these cases, only one of the partners in the marriage was canonized, and in each case it is only "celibate" practices, i.e. practices not unique to coupledom, which are described for our edification — such things as continence, hair shirts, hard beds, long hours of prayer, charity to the poor, penance done, revelations received, and convents founded.

## Married Mystics

When we look to married mystics, the fully celibate nature of our spiritual tradition is again confirmed. Some married mystics had too little sexual experience. The marriage of Paulinus of Nola (353-431), for example, was happy and lasted for 19 years until his wife's death, but the couple early took a vow of continence, after the miscarriage of their first child, and lived thenceforward like monastics ("Paulinus of Nola," in the *Encyclopédie des mystiques*, dir. M.M. Davy; Paris: R. Laffont, 1972). Others, like Ramon Lull (1232-1316), had too much, his marriage seeming to have made little difference to his pattern of promiscuity (cf. Kenneth Leech's introduction in *The Book of the Lover and Beloved*, tr. E. Allison Peers; New York: Paulist Press, 1978, p. 1). Still others were entirely unhappy. The French Roman Catholic, Marie Guyart (1599-1672), who became Marie de l'Incarnation, having had in a dream vision at age seven an embrace from Christ, who asked her "Will you be Mine?," married only at her parents' insistence, and for two years until her husband died showed "patience under the trial of married life" (*Word from New France: The Selected Letters of Marie de l'Incarnation,* tr. and ed. Joyce Marshall; Toronto: Oxford University Press, 1967, p. 55. Also *The Autobiography of the Venerable Marie of the Incarnation, O.S.U.: Mystic and Missionary,* tr. John J. Sullivan, S.J.; Chicago: Loyola University Press, 1964, p. 187).

But even when marriage was happy and of some length, sexual experience was seemingly unconnected to the spiritual life. Lack of common spiritual commitment was a factor in some cases. Elizabeth Seton (1774-1821), foundress of the American Sisters of Charity, married seemingly for love, but her intense piety was not shared by her husband. She wrote in one letter that "Willy does not understand"; in another that she was satisfied to have him gone on a trip; and to a friend contemplating remarriage: "The very best of these men . . . are so unruly and perplexing that nothing should induce a reasonable woman to wear the chains of two of them, and that's the plain English of matrimony" (Dec. 20, 1799; VI, 29, "to Julia," quoted in *Numerous Choirs: A Chronicle of Elizabeth Bayley Seton and her Spiritual Daughters,* ed. Ellin M. Kelly; Evansville, IN: Mater Dei Provincialate, 1981). It is thus not surprising that she writes only of Jesus, her heavenly spouse, and of solitary "sweet pauses in spirit when the body seems to be forgotten" (Sr. Marie Celeste, *The Intimate Friendships of Elizabeth Anne Bayley Seton, S.C.: First Native Born American Saint, 1774-1821*; New York: Alba House, 1989; p. 57).

In some cases, the historical context was itself clearly antagonistic to marriage. Gregory of Nyssa (c.330-c.394), for example, became a professor of rhetoric and lived until midlife with a well-regarded wife named Theosebia. Though he is reported to have written that "agape strained to intensity is called eros," being finally persuaded to become a priest, he joined his brother and friend in the monastic life and wrote *De Virginitate,* lamenting his exclusion from that most perfect of states ("Gregory of Nyssa," in *Encyclopédie des mystiques*).

Even in supposedly supportive settings, however, married mystics are silent about sexual ecstasy. The Puritans Sarah Pierrepoint and Jonathan Edwards, for example, both well advanced in the spiritual life, describe only mystical experiences of the traditional type, whether from reticence, from ignorance due to lack of conjugal models, or from some other cause, we do not know (*Jonathan Edwards: Basic Writings*, ed. Ola Elizabeth Winslow; New York: NAL Signet Classics, 1966; pp. 66-67, 81ff). We do know, of course, that structured spiritual counseling for couples has rarely been available, and that mystics are traditionally shy of publicizing their experience, usually doing so only at the insistence of directors or guides.

The most tantalizing example, held to be a model for the successful combination of marriage and the most advanced states of prayer, is the other Marie of the Incarnation (1566-1618), the mystic who was for 16 years Barbe Avrillot, for 31 Mme. Pierre Acarie, and for the final five years of her life, after the death of her husband, a Discalced Carmelite nun. Brought to the attention of the Capuchins because of her intense raptures, which continued for a period of four years, even during the birth of her sixth child, she became widely respected as a spiritual director and was judged a mystic according to the strictest definition.

Is she, finally, our model, married mystic? There was no doubt about her ecstatic experience, and no questioning the fact that it began not in her youth but six or seven years after her marriage. The fullness of her conjugal experience was denied, however, during the process for her beatification. A deposition maintained that hers was "a marriage of bodies, not hearts" (Lancelot C. Sheppard, *Barbe Acarie, Wife and Mystic: A Biography*; London: Burns and Oates, 1953; p. 159). Also a contemporary biographer declared that after "the urgent promptings of divine love felt at her spiritual awakening," she felt conflict between them and her bodily love for her husband (Sheppard, p. 37). In this view, her life merely gives an example of the spirit working in very adverse circumstances.

It is unfortunate that we know her only through these contemporary biases, for three other pieces of information call this interpretation of her life into question. First, her modern biographer notes that a spiritual advisor caused her great pain in prescribing that she behave coldly to her husband for a month (Sheppard, p. 55), a fact which strongly suggests that her heart was, despite official testimony, indeed engaged in her relation with her husband, and that the conflict between husband and God was perhaps not so much hers as her confessor's.

Second, her instruction on prayer was said to be in general Teresian, but abstract: advising direct union somewhat in the manner of the *Cloud of Unknowing* (Sheppard, p. 107), a teaching which would have been more compatible with the practice of sexual ecstasy than an approach to God either through ideas or through images.

And third is the fact that she burned the bulk of her writings on the spiritual life before her death, only a few short pieces of a traditional nature being spared (Sheppard, p. 200), leaving open the possibility they were not entirely of the prevailing orthodoxy, or perhaps even that they reflected on the spiritual dimensions of sexual relationship. This is sheer speculation, however, and on the available evidence, this mystic stands, like the others, as evidence that sex and mysticism are wholly unconnected.

# Appendix B

# Tidbits, Inspiring and Otherwise

---

Adamites: Early church practitioners of some sort of nudity, opposed by Epiphanius; according to Augustine, they practiced community of wives and promiscuity; some see twelfth-century French Waldensians (absolution by laity) as a continuation (now existing in France, Italy, Spain, and Switzerland).

Ambrose: Marriage "lower" but safer than vowed celibacy.

Anabaptists: Accepted polygamy in the sixteenth century. Because of individual spiritual responsibility, women are partners in mission.

Anselm: Eleventh-century doctor of the church who taught that marriage was a figure of the Trinity (creation, redemption, consummation).

Antony: My book, the Word of God, is the nature of created things.

Aquinas: Sense pleasure perfects, unsensuality is a defect; the ultimate end of man is served by games and delight; magnanimity is a virtue; the conjugal is the greatest possible human love.

Armenian practice: Interchange of crosses at betrothal.

Ars, Curé de: The love of God is like an overflowing current which sweeps everything in its course . . . The interior life is like a bath of love wherein one plunges.

Asclepius: The mystery and sexual intercourse are both accomplished in secret and involve intimate interaction. If you (sing.) wish to see the reality of this mystery, then you should see the wonderful representation of the intercourse that takes place between the male and the female. For when the semen reaches the climax, it leaps forth. In that moment the female receives the strength of the male and vice versa.

Athanasius: Forty verses on the Incarnation and the Trinity: "This is the Catholic Faith: We reverence with deepest awe One God in Trinity and Trinity in Unity. We do not mix together The Persons; Nor do we divide The Divine Being."

Atharveda: Collection of marriage charms, originally sacred doctrine, later *ars amandi.*

**B**ailey: The ends of sex in the Old Testament were unitive and procreative; in the New, unitive and analogical.

Barth: Sex is an image of kingdom, foretaste of beatitude, chief sacramental means of henosis, vehicle of Holy Spirit, sacred event leading to perfect union with the will of God, perhaps one of the primary means of spiritual grace.

Basil: "[You were] so united in your way of life . . . [that] parting was no less painful than if the half of your body was torn away."

Bernard (St.): Carnal love for self and others is the first step toward the love of God; the love of God, in this life, is carnal as well as spiritual.

Bernard (Jessie): Every marriage is two marriages — the man's and the woman's.

Bharati: The central sadhana of tantrism is the exercise of sexual contact under tantric laboratory conditions, mental or actual. "Right-handed" if with one's own wife; "left-handed" if with a *mahamudra* (consecrated female partner).

Birds: The neighbor is that person appointed by God to bring out the best in us.

Bonaventure: Every creature is divine word because it proclaims God. The world is an icon of God, a ladder to God. The Trinity is Father, Word, Love.

Bruckner: Sex is the space where limit is pulverized, two mingle without destroying each other.

Buber: Whoever stands in relation participates in a being that is neither merely a part of him nor merely outside him.

Bucer: Placed companionship before procreation in listing the purposes of marriage.

Buddhism: There were married monks in Kashmir in 500 A.D. and in Tibet in the eighth century.

Bynum (Caroline): "The theme of the positive religious significance of physicality runs throughout 13th-century theology."

Caesarius of Arles: Do not go east to find charity, sail west to find devotion. It is within you. God put within us that which he expects of us.

Calvin: Taught Christians to conquer the world, not withdraw from it; sex itself is holy and honorable, but sexual pleasure, because "immoderate," is still evil, and virginity, if freely chosen, a superior state.

Capon: The couple is a created reflection of the coinherence of God.

Caussade: Cultivate the sacrament of the present moment.

Chalcedonian Creed (similar to latter part of Athanasian Creed, 451): Christ is one in two natures, a union without blurring of persons.

Chaldean literature: In the nuptial chamber, the spouse is like a tree of life whose fruits nourish and whose leaves heal.

Chavasse: Jesus Christ is the Bride and the Groom, one-flesh.

Chögyam Trungpa: The Shambhala warrior renounces anything that is a barrier between himself and others.

Christine of Pisa: Medieval poet who refused to separate marriage and romance.

Comedy: Originating in archaic fertility ceremonies, its structure is a movement from struggle to reconciliation and celebration.

Clement of Alexandria: Evening is the proper time for "the mystic rites of nature." The partner should be similar in all respects, and not be compelled by force. Pleasure (if for its own sake, sin) is an expression of and the chief means of achieving unity; like the Eucharist, it makes Christian community.

Cloud of Unknowing: The stirring of love and desire constitute the life of spirit. Advocates spontaneous one-syllable prayer.

Columban: Happy is he who dies of love.

Confucius: In the long run, the passions and feelings are more trustworthy than human principles of right and wrong.

Deschene: Sex is a mysterious bond between heaven and earth, an occasion and opportunity for celebration; a holy means of encounter, a dimension in which God shares with couple.

Donne, John (married English priest and poet): First to use the word sex as conjugal intercourse; first hymn to the new breed of holy persons. Love and sex not ascent into incorporeal rapture but descent into psychosomatic unity. The presence of the spouse in self intensifies not annihilates individualism. Ecstasy à deux.

Douglas and Slinger: In the Tantric tradition commitment must be preceded by serious effort and is itself an opening into potency. "The fear of mysticism has only been overshadowed by the fear of the inherent liberating power of human sexuality."

Dürckheim: Touch, the most intense human encounter, provides contact with the other and through him to life.

Early Christian imagery: Paradise, bird (phoenix and nightingale), courtly and conjugal love.

Eckhart: If we lack, we desire; if we possess, we love.

Ephrem the Syriac: "O Lord, inflame these lovers with the fire of love; in the morning of all your days, may you awake unto joy."

Epiphanius, son of Carpocrates: The righteousness of God is communion with equality. Desire is the first will of God.

Esoteric Tantrism (assimilated into Indian thought in the fourth century): Union with The One Reality is symbolically expressed by the union of the deity and his consort.

Everard, John: The Holy Spirit is an act of love between the Father and the Son.

Falk and Gross: For Saraha (Tibetan Buddhist), further spiritual progress was blocked until he married.

Goergan: Christian marriage is as "abnormal" as celibacy. Though easily naturalized, it is not the cultural standard.

Gospel of Thomas: Where there are two or one, I am with him. If two make peace with each other in this one house they will say to the mountain, "move away," and it will move away. When you make the two one, you will become the sons of man, you will enter the kingdom.

Greeley: Sex is an untamable power, most constructive in marriage. Less than exciting sex is infidelity.

Groote: Marriage and celibacy are of equivalent value.


Hasidim: God is imminent in all existence. The earthly is an allegory of the heavenly passion. The rabbi and his wife in union are like Adam and Eve before they sinned, their bedroom like paradise. The first of the virtues is *hitlahavut,* the fire of ecstasy.

Haughton: There is no society in which normal "domestic" sex has been seriously regarded as sacramental by ordinary people . . . Married sex is not only a possible setting for a truly spiritual love, but also the most likely one.

Hendrix, Harville (founder of Imago Relationship therapy): Conscious co-operation with the unconscious forces that create the dyad.

Hernnhut: Lutheran familial monastery under Papa (God the Father), Mama (the Holy Spirit) and Brother (Jesus).

Heywood, Carter: In the context of relational mutuality and fidelity, sex is not only right. It is sacred. It is sacramental, an "outward, visible sign" of the power and love of God.

Hilary of Poitiers: The married who pray together are like the Trinity.

von Hildebrand: Sex celebrates the holiness of interpersonal relationship, celebrates love and effects what it signifies.

Hort: The senses may become instruments of deliverance.

Hoyland: Speaks of the mystical experience as *usus amoris*, with sexual imagery so strong and realistic that Leclerq terms it "hardly translatable."

Hume (Basil): Marital experience is a *fons theologica.*

Irenaeus of Lyons: The glory of God is the glory of people fully alive.

Islam (medieval): Sex is an act of worship; precede it with prayer and wash ritually after.

Isocrates: Marriage is the most comprehensive kind of *koinonia*.

Jamaa of Congo: African movement interpreting the Bible sexually, founded by Belgian priest.

*James*: "Confess and pray mutually" (5:13).

Jennings, Elizabeth: The Fall was a disordering of mutuality.

John of the Cross: Love effects a likeness between the Lover and the Beloved.

Johnston (William): All other virtues, says Thomas Aquinas, following Aristotle, are found in the golden mean; but we cannot love too much.

Jovinian: Abstinence and food taken with thanks are equal.

Kabbala: Sex is the restoration of the image of God.

Kohlbenschlag: Conjugal soul-making is choreographic.

Kundalini yoga: Method of transforming physical energy into spiritual by concentration rather than sublimation.

Lanzo des Vasto: God is in the union of those who unite.

Brother Lawrence: Prayer is the practice of the presence of God.

Lindbergh: A good relationship has a pattern like a dance, and some of the same rules.

Luther: Moved the school of sanctity from the monastery to the home, calling marriage the true way to life everlasting but also a kind of hospital for the sick, the necessary antidote for man's incontinence. Sex, inevitable with propinquity, was still unclean. The one-flesh is a sacramental image of God by analogy.

**M**acarius of Alexandria: Be led by desire in following God. Virginity and marriage are of equal merit.

Maimonides: Aim a little beyond the strictly right.

Maximus the Confessor: The love of God and man are not two, but two aspects of single total love.

Mead (Margaret): The American marriage ideal is . . . one of the most difficult marriage forms that the human race has ever attempted.

Medieval theology: Truth and love both come from the Primal Lover, the mover of the universe.

Meeks: The symbol of the androgyne is a rejection of the existing order.

Merezhkovskii: Russian novelist and critic whose eros mysticism fuses classical ideas with Christian thought.

Monden: In love an invitation may be more binding than an order, coolness more wounding than betrayal.

**N**ahman of Bratslav: Author of *Tikkun ha-kelali*, reportedly the last in an entire line of Kabbalistic literature (beginning with the *Holy Letter*) devoted to the sexual life and practices.

Nédoncelle: Suffering intervenes to warn loving persons of a deficiency of their work.

Nelson: Sexual sin is alienation from our divinely intended sexuality.

New Catholic Encyclopedia: Marriage is a special call to holiness and serves a supernatural function in the Mystical Body of Christ.

**O**neida Community: Perfectionists with an egalitarian religious ethos, practicing Biblical communism, mutual criticism, pantagamy (not free love, but "complex marriage," with elaborate rules and sanctions).

Ong, Walter: Man knows truth only by binarism of intellection, by pairing (*The flower is red; The bird flies*).

Oresme: Sex is natural and divine; take the trouble to develop it.

**P**aphnutius: Early hermit who influenced the Council of Nicea to reject absolute clerical celibacy.

Paul VI: Sex is the basis of the spiritual impulse toward the infinite, a means of expression, knowledge and communion, a sign of Christ and the church.

Peck: The principle work of love is attention.

Pelz: The ritual recurrence of the erotic pattern re-awakens spontaneous love. In a society governed almost exclusively by impersonal and often inhuman considerations, marriage offers some of the few remaining chances to become human and humane.

*I Peter*: "Treat your wives with consideration. This will stop anything from coming in the way of your prayers" (3:7).

Porter, Katherine Ann: Marriage is the art of belonging.

Priscillianism: Second-century movement which admitted of God in feminine form.

**R**amsey, Michael: Mystical experience is given to some, contemplation is for all.

Rolle: *Calor, dulcor, canor* (fire, sweetness, song).

Roman catechism (1566): Procreation is not a necessary part of marriage.

**S**arum rite (1549): Marriage is "a unique kind of unity, at first formal, then increasingly actual."

Shakers: Egalitarian celibates who taught that God was Mother and Father and that redemption was to be found in making good bread.

Sheehy: Couples, who communicate on the average twenty-seven minutes a week, exchange the most words on their third date and in the year before divorce.

Shepherd of Hermas: There are pleasures that are able to save people.

Spurgeon: Marital sex is a spiritual encounter whose ultimate goal is discovery of the presence of God.

Talmud: Three things have in themselves something of the beyond — the sun, the sabbath, and sexual union.

Tantra: The male and female in embrace are a copy of the cosmic unity.

Teilhard de Chardin: Human sexuality is a fundamental force providing the basis for any other human love, including the love of God and that form of love which finds expression in charity. The goal is integration toward unification, humanization, spiritualization.

TeSelle: Eros is the basis of metaphor, the way humans discover.

Theophan the Recluse: Bind the mind with one thought.

Thornton, Martin: Why link only pain, and not Cana, to Christ?


Upanishads: The Lord of Creatures creates by sexual intercourse, giving instructions for procreation with the invocation of Vishnu and other gods.


Weil, Simone: To reproach mystics with loving God by means of the faculty of sexual love is as though one were to reproach a painter with making pictures by means of colours composed of material substances. We don't have anything else with which to love.

Weiner: Marriage is a circular action-reaction system.

Whiteheads: Conjugal discipline is confrontation, conversation, and love-making.


Yeats: We believe only thoughts which have been conceived not in the brain but in the whole body.


Zaehner: Blasphemy is not in the comparison [of mystical and sexual ecstasy] but in degrading the one act of which man is capable that makes him like God both in the intensity of his union with his partner and in the fact that by this union he is a co-creator with God.

Zeno of Verona: "Like a skilled coachman you harmonize by these tender loins those who submit their yet inexperienced necks to the very holy yoke of marriage so that their effort may be equal in labor and affection." (Serm. 1.4)

# Annotated Bibliography

## A. Theological Sources and Resources

Aelred of Rievaulx. *Spiritual Friendship*, tr. Mary Eugenia Laker (Kalamazoo, MI: Cistercian Publications, 1974). Love for friend is of same kind as love in *Song of Songs* and the love for God. See also the full-length study for nonspecialized audience by Brian Patrick McGuire, *Brother and Lover: Aelred of Rievault* (New York: Crossroad, 1994).

Baelz, Peter. *Prayer and Providence: A Background Study* (New York: Seabury Press, 1968). Reflections by a Cambridge don on use of personal language of divine activity and purpose.

Bailey, D(errick) S(herwin), *The Mystery of Love and Marriage: A Study in the Theology of Sexual Relation* (New York: Harper & Brothers, 1952). Preliminary theology of sexual relation based on the Biblical concept of "one-flesh." *The Man-Woman (Sexual) Relation in Christian Thought* (New York: Harper & Row, 1959). Historical review of Church's attitude toward sexual relation as basis for a theology of sex.

Barry, William A. and William J. Connolly. *The Practice of Spiritual Direction* (New York: Seabury Press, 1983). Introduction to spiritual direction of individuals having affective experiences of God.

Berman, Morris. *Coming to Our Senses: Body and Spirit in the Hidden History of the West* (New York: Simon and Schuster, 1989). Argues the crucial importance of sensory input (lost in the age of binary classification) and the value of the marginal, the ambiguous, the anomaly (bodily fluids, disorder, the other) which need to be "composted" back into society.

Bonsirven, J. *Palestinian Judaism in the Time of Jesus Christ*, tr. William Wolf (New York: Harper & Row, 1964). According to Hillel, union becomes a religious act by consecration; wedding-going is meritorious.

Boyer, Ernest Jr., *Finding God at Home: Family Life as Spiritual Discipline* (San Francisco: Harper & Row, 1988). The edge and the center, spiritualities of the individual and the group. Two pages on marriage.

Buber, Martin, *I and Thou*, tr. Walter Kaufmann (New York: Charles Scribner's Sons, 1937). Dedicated to his wife Paula, "the abyss and the light of the world," helped shift the locus of value from the singular to the plural.

Cady, Linell E. "Relational Love: A Feminist Christian Vision," in *Embodied Love: Sensuality and Relationship as Feminist Values*, Paula M. Cooey, Sharon A. Farmer and Mary Ellen Ross, eds. (San Francisco: Harper & Row, 1987). Extends the tradition to make normative the "mutual cocreation of self and community through the spirit of love" and to define the divine as "the unifying of being."

Caffarel, Henri. *Marriage is Holy* (Chicago: Fides, 1963, c1957). Early classic by one of the prime exponents of the conjugal movement in France.

Chavasse, Claude. *The Bride of Christ: An Enquiry into the Nuptial Element in Early Christianity* (London: Faber and Faber Ltd., 1940). Biblical study mainly documenting the traditional Christ/Church metaphor, but noting also the pre-exilic worship of Yahweh, which included a Divine Consort.

Crespy, George, Paul Evdokimov, and Christian Duquoc. *Marriage and Christian Tradition* (Techny, IL: Divine Word Publications, 1968). Theologians from three traditions reexamine the institution.

Cunningham, Lawrence. *The Meaning of Saints* (New York: Harper & Row, 1980). More general and updated English equivalent of Delooz' work, also concluding that few married men and women were canonized, none of whom could serve as models for conjugal sanctity. Calls for a new vision.


Davis, Charles. *Body as Spirit: The Nature of Religious Feeling* (New York: Seabury Press, 1976). Ex-priest explores the connections between emotion and mysticism.

Déchanet, J.-M. *Christian Yoga* (New York: Harper & Row, 1960). Practical introduction by French Benedictine (advice for women not always accurate).

Delooz, Pierre. *Sociologie et Canonisations*. (La Haye: Martinus Nihoff, 1969). Early exhaustive study of canonization, the geographical origins of the saints and their roles in life.

Derrick, Christopher. *Sex and Sacredness: A Catholic Homage to Venus* (San Francisco, CA: Ignatius Press, 1982). Description of Easter Vigil as performed for many centuries, emphasizing its incarnational, male and female aspects.

Deschene, James M. "Sexuality: Festival of the Spirit," *Studies in Formative Spirituality* 2:1, p. 28. Sexuality as bond between heaven and earth is an occasion for celebration. Lack of thrill is a lack of seeing as God sees.

Dessesprit, Albert. *Le mariage un sacrement* (Paris: Le Centurion, 1981). Unsatisfactory search for Biblical models for marriage.

Dürckheim, Karlfried Graf. *Meditieren, wozu und wie* (Freiburg im Breisgau, Verlag Herder, 1976). Transformation of self to manifest divine being in the world.

Dyckman, Katherine Marie, and L. Patrick Carroll. *Inviting the Mystic: Supporting the Prophet: An Introduction to Spiritual Direction* (New York: Paulist Press, 1981). Extends definition of prayer to include all of life.


Egan, Harvey D. *Christian Mysticism: The Future of a Tradition* (New York: Pueblo Publishing Company, 1984). Jesuit examines

Biblical mysticism and six mystics, concluding that more work is needed to relate the stages of mystical ascent and contemporary life-cycle psychologies.

Evdokimov, Paul. *Sacramental Love: The Nuptial Mystery in the Light of Orthodox Tradition* (Crestwood, NY: St. Vladimir's Seminary Press, 1985). Compares the married and monastic states, and presents married love as a sacrament and a royal priesthood.

Evola, Julius. *The Metaphysics of Sex* (London: East-West Publications, 1983). In-depth scholarly study of erotic experience and the esoteric dyad, as illuminated by ancient traditions and myths.

Fontaine, Jacques. "The Practice of Christian Life: The Birth of the Laity," in *Christian Spirituality: Origins to the Twelfth Century,* eds. Bernard McGinn and Jean Meyendorff (New York: Crossroad, 1985). Review of the early centuries.

Foster, Lawrence. *Religion and Sexuality: The Shakers, the Mormons, and the Oneida Community* (Chicago: University of Illinois Press, 1984). The millennial impulse and the creation of alternative family systems, complex marriage and polygamy.

Fox, Matthew, ed. *Western Spirituality: Historical Roots, Ecumenical Routes* (Notre Dame, Indiana: Fides/Claretian, 1979). *Original Blessing: A Primer in Creation Spirituality* (Santa Fe, NM: Bear & Co., 1983). Jubilant panentheism, congenial to conjugal spirituality. God in us and us in God, trust of body, imagination, cosmos. Via Positiva, Via Negativa, Via Creativa, and Via Transformativa (by acting out of interdependence).

Fuchs, Eric. *Sexual Desire and Love: Origins and History of the Christian Ethic of Sexuality and Marriage*, tr. Marsha Daigle (New York: Seabury Press, 1983). French Protestant minister constructs a theology of marriage, using Biblical and historical sources.

Gardella, Peter. *Innocent Ecstasy: How Christianity Gave America an Ethic of Sexual Pleasure* (New York: Oxford University Press, 1985). The evolution of Catholic teaching on sensuality. American Christianity has helped create our hopes for a guiltless and salvific sexual life.

Garrigou-Lagrange, Rég(inald). *The Three Ages of the Interior Life: Prelude of Eternal Life*, tr. Sister M. Timothea Doyle (St. Louis: B. Herder Book Company, 1947-1948). Classic treatise of systematic theology by French Dominican.

Goergan, Donald. *The Sexual Celibate* (Garden City, NY: Image/Doubleday, 1979). Theological and psychological insights into tactility and intimacy for the celibate, and the "abnormality" and eschatological dimension of Christian marriage.

Gordan, David Cole. *Self-Love* (New York: Macmillan, 1970). History of disapproval of masturbation, study of it as experience of unification, comparing it with other producers of peak experience, such as mountain climbing, sports, business, food and drugs.

Greeley, Andrew M. *Ecstasy: A Way of Knowing* (Englewood Cliffs, NJ: Prentice-Hall, 1974). The sexual is similar to the mystical. *Sexual Intimacy* (New York: Seabury, 1973). Priest-sociologist's perception of the power of sex. Lovers' wiles are the way God works on us.

Green, Elmer E., Alyce M. Green, and E. Dale Walters. "Voluntary control of internal states: psychology and physiology," in *The Journal of Transpersonal Psychology*, No. 1 (1970), pp. 1-27. Laboratory investigations of meditative states at the Menninger Foundation.

Gregg, Richard B. *Spirit through Body*, (New York: J. B. Lippencott, 1956). Sex as aid to meditation, means toward unitive knowing and symbolic union with God (transcending pairs of opposites lifts into spiritual). Morning after, meditation. Dangers (self-deception, rationalization of lust, end not means)' and difficulties (attachment, distraction).

Grelot, Pierre. *Le Couple Humain dans l'Écriture* (Paris: Éditions du Cerf, 1969). Leans heavily on St. Paul's "divided heart."

Guigo II. *The Ladder of Monks: A Letter on the Contemplative Life, and Twelve Meditations*, tr. Edmund Colledge and James Walsh (Garden City, NY: Doubleday/Image, 1978). Modern English translation, with critical introduction and commentary, of classics ascribed to the prior of a French Carthusian monastery. The spiritual life as *ludus amoris*, a game or struggle of love, the spouse visiting and withdrawing.

Haughton, Rosemary. *Love* (Baltimore, MD: Penguin, 1971). Literate essays on desire, devotion, mysticism and friendship, with the perspective that ordinary married sex is sacramental. *Theology of Marriage* (Butler, WI: Clergy Book Service, 1971). Short work by Anglo-American Roman Catholic laywoman presenting tradition and current thought. Author of *The Mystery of Sexuality* (New York: Paulist Press, 1972).

Hocking. *The Meaning of God in Human Experience: A Philosophic Study of Religion* (New Haven: Yale University Press, 1912). Love is a paradigm and source of ordinary mystical experience; isolation is an illusion.

Holland, John M., ed., *Religion and Sexuality: Judaic-Christian Viewpoints in the U.S.A.* (San Francisco: The Association of Sexologists, 1981). Substantial contributions from each of the religious traditions represented.

Holmes, Urban T. III *The History of Christian Spirituality: An Analytical Introduction* (New York: Seabury Press, 1980). Chronology introduced by short essay on the nature of prayer. *Spirituality for Ministry* (San Francisco: Harper and Row, 1982). Sex and spirituality are closely related. Sex is a sacramental means of effecting the whole man: an expression of the ineffable, like prayer, makes the marital bond like Eucharist, and creates Christian community.

*The Holy Letter: A Study in Medieval Jewish Sexual Morality (Iggeret ha-kodesh,* 13th-century Kabbala; first published 1546), ed. and trans. Seymour J. Cohen (NY: KTAV Pub. House, 1976). "The way in which a man may consummate sexual union with his wife so that it will be for the sake of heaven."

Horner, Tom. *Sex in the Bible* (Rutland, VT: Charles E. Tuttle Company, Inc., 1974). Nonscholarly survey. One man's view.

Hunter, David G., tr. & ed. *Marriage in the Early Church* (Minneapolis: Fortress Press, 1992). Useful translations of primary Greek and Latin sources with an introduction.

James, William. *The Varieties of Religious Experience* (New York: The New American Library, 1958). Famous classic on the psychology of religion, identifying "once-born" and "twice-born" religious types and defining mysticism and saintliness.

Johnston, William. *The Still Point: Reflections on Zen & Christian Mysticism* (New York: Harper & Row, 1970). Disciplined meditators become physiologically different. An intuitive communion beyond words, a fusion of consciousnesses can exist in deeply spiritual contact between lovers. *Silent Music: The Science of Meditation* (New York: Harper/Perennial Lib., 1974). Love leads to the mind-expansion of the great religions, *samadhi* without words. *The Mirror Mind: Spirituality and Transformation* (San Francisco: Harper & Row, 1981). A section on the relation of eros and agape.

Jung, Carl Gustav. *Psychology and Religion* (New Haven: Yale University Press, 1938). Much-quoted work advocating the importance of the "shadow side" of self and predicting that the West would develop its own brand of yoga based in Christianity.

Kern, Louis J. *An Ordered Love: Sex Roles and Sexuality in Victorian Utopias — The Shakers, the Mormons, and the Oneida Community* (Chapel Hill: University of North Carolina Press, 1981). Alternatives (celibacy, polygamy, pantagamy) to the traditional role of women and to the dyadic form of marriage, seen as hypocritical patriarchal tyranny.

Kirk, K(enneth) E. *The Vision of God: The Christian Doctrine of the Summum Bonum* (New York: Harper Torchbooks, 1966). Anglican moral theologian on the history of Christian religious discipline as conflict between the "humanist" (world-embracing) and the rigorist (world-renouncing), explaining the ordinary/perfect (married/celibate) distinction as being created to allow these two worldviews to coexist.

Kosnick, Anthony, et al. *Human Sexuality* (New York: Paulist/Newman, 1977). Roman Catholic scholars conclude that ethical sex is self-liberating, other-enriching, honest, faithful, socially responsible, life-serving, and joyous. Emphasizes Augustine's positive views on marriage.

Lamm, Maurice. *The Jewish Way in Love and Marriage* (San Francisco: Harper & Row, 1980). Rabbi synthesizes the traditional values of Jewish marriage.

Leclercq, Jean. *Monks on Marriage: A Twelfth-Century View* (New York: Seabury Press, 1982). Finds positive attitudes toward marriage, but few hints of distinctively conjugal holiness: Ida of Lorraine and Eustache, count of Boulogne, played together with their children and dealt jointly with the financial and administrative affairs of their domain (but Ida of Herzfeld felt love for God in the sexual act and so "tempered her expressions of love").

Leites, Edmund. *The Puritan Conscience and Modern Sexuality* (New Haven: Yale University Press, 1986). Study of the great age of Puritan writings on marriage from 1620 to 1660, including a short history of friendship from Aristotle on to that time.

Liguori, Alphonsus. *Theologia Moralis.* An encyclopedic work by Redemptorist (1697-1787) who was declared Doctor of the Church in 1871. He argues from natural law that couples have an obligation to pursue orgasm.

May, Gerald. *Care of Mind/Care of Spirit* (San Francisco: Harper & Row, 1982). Spiritual and sexual awakening are linked, but the spiritual journey is private, involving levels of experience that cannot be shared. In marriage, neither sufficient perspective nor adequate freedom of attentiveness exists for one to be director to the other.

Merton, Thomas. *Seeds of Contemplation* (New York: Dell, 1949). "The kind of book that writes itself almost automatically in a monastery."

Miles, Margaret. *Fullness of Life: Historical Foundations for a New Asceticism* (Philadelphia: Westminster Press, 1981). The incarnation and the resurrection require a view of the human which integrates the body.

Mollenkott, Virginia Ramey. *Sensuous Spirituality: Out from Fundamentalism* (New York: Crossroad, 1992). Evangelical lesbian feminist's look at eros in the Bible and the tradition.

Moorman, John R. H. *The Anglican Spiritual Tradition* (Springfield, Illinois: Templegate Publishers, 1983). Standard history of Anglican spirituality.


Nachmanides. *The Commentary on Genesis, Chapters 1-6* (Leiden: E.J. Brill, 1960). Sex is pure and holy; God is with man and woman in sex. At the end, they will account for all legitimate pleasures not enjoyed.

Nédoncelle, Maurice. *God's Encounter with Man: A Contemporary Approach to Prayer*, tr. Am Manson (New York: Sheed & Ward, 1964). Prayer is an expression of bonding, human prayer the basis for thinking about divine prayer. *Love and the Person*, tr. Sister Ruth Adelaide (New York: Sheed & Ward, 1966). Interpersonal philosophy based on the I-Thou relationship, but jumping from one to the group.

Needleman, Carla. "Falling Towards Grace" in *Studia Mystica* V,1 (Spring, 1982). Vivid description of ecstasy understanding in body, not mind.

Nelson, James B. *Embodiment: An Approach to Sexuality and Christian Theology* (Minneapolis: Augsburg Publishing House, 1978). The most thorough statement of current theological opinion on sexuality (an incarnational stance). Sex education, therapy, and liturgy necessary. Cf. also "Toward a Theology of Human Sexuality" ch. V in Holland.


O'Brien, Elmer. *Varieties of Mystic Experience* (New York: Mentor-Omega, 1965). Discussion of generic mystical experience and its literary form, with excerpts and introductions.


Pagels, Elaine. *The Gnostic Gospels* (New York: Vintage Books, 1979). The complexity of early Christian movement revealed in the Nag Hammadi texts calls Gnosticism as heresy into question. *Adam, Eve, and the Serpent* (New York: Random House, 1988). Ideas on sexuality, moral freedom, and human value took definitive form during the first four centuries and continue to affect our culture.

Parrinder, Geoffrey. *Mysticism in the World's Religions* (New York: Oxford Press, 1976). Unity between two humans is a sacred symbol of the spiritual unity of divine beings. *Sex in World's Religions* (London: Sheldon Press, 1980). Easily readable summary of customs in the major religions of the world.

Phipps, William E. *Recovering Biblical Sensuousness* (Philadelphia: Westminster Press, 1975). One of several provocative books in the area of sexuality. Others on the sexuality of Jesus, and on the positions of influential theologians such as Augustine, Milton and John Donne on the subject of women. "Is Paul's Attitude Toward Sexual Relations Contained in I Cor. 7.1?," *New Testament Studies*, vol. 28, pp. 125-131, denies Paul's supposed denigration of sexual intercourse, attributing it to Paul's patristic and monastic interpreters.

Pittenger, Norman. *Making Sexuality Human* (Philadelphia: Pilgrim Press, 1970). Look for the image of God in the self-as-lover, the capacity for love.

Ruether, Rosemary Radford. *Women of Spirit: Female Leadership in the Jewish & Christian Traditions,* ed. Rosemary Ruether & Eleanor McLaughlin (New York: Simon and Schuster, 1979). Gnostics and Shakers believed in the androgyny of God. Christ-church symbolism in Puritanism (where marriage is the norm) reinforces hierarchy of sexual roles. Prisca's dream: Christ as female figure saying this is a holy place and here would Jerusalem descend out of heaven. *Womanguides: Readings Toward a Feminist Theology* (Boston: Beacon Press, 1985). Invaluable texts from many traditions.

Schillebeeckx, E. *Marriage: Secular Reality and Saving Mystery* (London, Sheed and Ward, 1965). Vol. 1 "Marriage in the Old and New Testaments." Vol. 2 "Marriage in the History of the Church." Interesting study by a leading Dominican Theologian. Unfortunately, his volume of anthropological analysis never appeared.

Shideler, Mary McDermott. *The Theology of Romantic Love: A Study in the Writings of Charles Williams* (New York: Harper & Brothers, 1962). Classic study of co-inherence and "the way of exchange."

Slade, Herbert. *Exploration into Contemplative Prayer* (New York: Paulist, 1975). Advocate of transforming physical energy into spiritual insight by movement and breathing. Includes forms of ritual. *Contemplative Intimacy* (London: Darton Longman and Todd, 1977). Fruit of Anchorhold, a religious community exploring new forms of prayer and community life. Includes training exercises.

Soloviev, Vladimir Sergeevich. *The Meaning of Love*, tr. Jane Marshall (London: Geoffrey Bles-The Centenary Press, 1945). *A Soloviev Anthology,* ed. S. I. Frank, tr. N. Duddington (London, 1950). Eastern Orthodox theologian holding celibacy to be *angelosis;* marriage, the restoration of the *imago,* divinization, androgyny, and *theosis.* Amor aequalis is the necessary basis of spiritual growth, making a new man in as radical an evolutionary leap as from reason to anima. Cf. also Strémooukhoff, D. *Vladimir Soloviev and His Messianic Work,* tr. Elizabeth Meyendorff, ed. Phillip Guilbeau and Heather Elise MacGregor (Belmont, MA: Nordland Publ., 1980).

Stevenson, Kenneth. *Nuptial Blessing: A Study of Christian Marriage Rites* (London, Alcuin Club/SPCK, 1982). Disputes the common assumption that no early Christian marriage rite existed.

Taylor, Jeremy. (1613-1667). *The Rule and Exercises of Holy Living* (Cleveland: World Publishing Company, 1956). First and most popular work. Either desire for procreation, avoidance of fornication, mutual endearment or "lightening and easing the cares and sadnesses of household affairs" must be present to legitimate desire. *Doctor Dubitantium, or the Rule of Conscience* (London: James Flesher, 1660). "Virginity is not more holy than chaste marriage." Sex acceptable during menstruation and pregnancy (vs. Leviticus and Jerome).

Timmerman, Joan H. *The Mardi Gras Syndrome: Re-thinking Christian Sexuality* (New York: Crossroad Publishing Company, 1984). *Sexuality and Spiritual Growth* (New York: Crossroad, 1992). Sexuality is a new source of religious experience which produces effects in the spiritual order. Advocates living out its potential as spiritual journey.

Trible, Phyllis. *God and the Rhetoric of Sexuality* (Philadelphia: Fortress Press, 1978). Explores female imagery for God, and the "image of God" in human sexuality as represented in Genesis 2-3, the Song of Songs, and the book of Ruth.

Ulanov, Ann Belford, Barry Ulanov, Philip Turner, et al. *Men and Women: Sexual Ethics in Turbulent Times* (Cambridge, MA: Cowley Publications, 1989). Collection of essays with a conservative point of view.

United Church of Christ. *Human Sexuality: A Preliminary Study* (New York: The United Church Press, 1977). The self experiences resurrection of the body in realizing unity, i.e. reconciling of body and mind, self and world. Spiritual growth is in increased freedom, sensuousness, love, and androgyny. Ethical standards: physical experience appropriate to the level of loving commitment; genital expression evaluated in terms of motive (love) and good intention. Good sex is erotic, warm, intimate, playful, immensely pleasurable; at times almost mystical in its possibilities of communication and communion leading to a sense of wholeness, of being at one with self, other, and God.

Watts, Alan. *Nature, Man, and Woman* (New York: Vintage Books, 1970). Discussion of Chinese Taoism, kundalini yoga, and the Christian potential for developing conjugal love as a means to the contemplative life.

Whitehead, Evelyn Eaton & James D. *Marrying Well: Possibilities in Christian Marriage Today* (Garden City, NY: Doubleday, 1981). Roman Catholic longitudinal examination of conjugal path. Sex celebrates holiness of interpersonal relationship; it is a making of and a sign of more love. *A Sense of Sexuality: Christian Love and Intimacy* (New York: Doubleday/Image, 1989). Social, historical, theological and psychological understandings illustrated with first-person anecdotes and examples from Scripture.

Yelchaninov, Alexander. "Fragments of a Diary" (1881-1934) in *A Treasury of Russian Spirituality*, ed. G. P. Fedotov (New York: Harper, 1950, 1965). Earthly life, particularly marriage, is a real reflection of the invisible, a complete transformation of man. Sex is the highest disclosure of human personality, achievement of plenitude.

Zaehner, Robert Charles. *Mysticism Sacred and Profane* (London: Oxford University Press, 1961). Mystical raptures closely akin to sex union, soul female, God male. Blasphemy not in comparison of sex and ecstasy but in degrading the one act of which man is capable that makes him like God, both in intensity of union with partner and in the fact that by this union he is a cocreator with God.

## Historical Studies

Brown, Peter. *The Body and Society: Men, Women, and Sexual Renunciation in Early Christianity* (New York: Columbia University Press, 1988).

Schillebeeckx, E. *Marriage: Secular Reality and Saving Mystery* (London: Sheed & Ward, 1965). Vol. 1: Marriage in the Old and New Testaments. Vol. 2: Marriage in the History of the Church.

# B. The Couple

Association of Couples for Marriage Enrichment, 459 S. Church St., P.O. Box 10596, Winston-Salem, NC.

National Marriage Encounter, 955 Lake Drive, St. Paul, MN 55120.

Bach, George R. and Peter Wyden. *The Intimate Enemy: How to Fight Fair in Love and Marriage* (New York: Avon Books, 1968). One of the best, along with Bach, George R. and Ronald M. Deutsch. *Pairing: How to Achieve Genuine Intimacy* (New York: Avon Books, 1970).

Barbeau, Clayton C. *Creative Marriage in the Middle Years* (New York: Seabury, 1976). Practical advice on need for selfing; fidelity as creation.

Berzon, Betty. *Permanent Partners: Building Gay and Lesbian Relationships That Last* (New York: E.P. Dutton, 1988). Practical approach to the same interpersonal probleMA faced by heterosexual pairs, plus the lack of visible role models, informed guidance, and societal support.

Blood, Robert O., Jr. and Donald M. Wolfe. *Husbands and Wives: The Dynamics of Married Living* (New York: The Free Press, 1960). Sociologist's analysis of marital habits in general and sexual behavior in particular, with cross-section samples and comparative data.

Clinebell, Charlotte H. and Harold J. *Intimate Marriage* (New York: Harper & Row, 1970). Methodist counseling for intentional marriage.

Denton, Wallace and Juanita Holt Denton. *Creative Couples: The Growth Factor in Marriage* (Philadelphia: Westminster Press, 1982). Based on their experiences in the marriage enrichment movement and current research. Appendix contains questions and exercises relating to each chapter.

Grace, Drs. Mike and Joyce. *A Joyful Meeting: Sexuality in Marriage* (St. Paul, MN. 55120: International Marriage Encounter, 955 Lake Drive, 1980). Simple language on the relationship between sex and love, patterns of response in intercourse, the fear-failure cycle, subtle gender differences, and variations in sexual appetites.

Josselson, Ruthellen. *The Space Between Us: Exploring the Dimensions of Human Relationships* (San Francisco: Jossey-Bass Publishers, 1992). Useful beginning in establishing a discourse of relatedness not based in psychopathology.

Keirsey, David and Marilyn Bates. *Please Understand Me* (Del Mar, CA: Promethean Nemesis, 1984). Sixteen different character and temperament types. Includes self-test.

Lasswell, Marcia and Norman M. Lobsenz. *No-Fault Marriage* (New York: Ballantine Books, 1976). Popular level self-help. *Styles of Loving: Why You Love the Way You Do* (Garden City, NY: Doubleday, 1980). Nonjudgmental approach to affectional differences based on Meyers-Briggs personality analysis.

Lederer, William J. and Don D. Jackson. *The Mirages of Marriage* (New York: Norton, 1968). Old, but still one of the best.

Leonard, George. *The End of Sex: Erotic Love After the Sexual Revolution* (Los Angeles: J.P. Tarcher, 1983). New Age explorer discovers "High Monogamy."

Mace, David and Vera. *How to Have a Happy Marriage* (New York: Ace Books, 1977). Program demanding 1-2 hours Sat-Sun and 1/2-1 hour M-F for 6 weeks. *Sacred Fire: Christian Marriage Through the Ages* (Nashville: Abingdon, 1986). Sturdy Quaker good sense.

O'Neill, Nena and George. *Open Marriage: A New Life Style for Couples* (New York: Avon, 1972). Book which challenged stereotypical roles and boundaries for marriage, widely but wrongly, according to its authors, understood as a call for sexual promiscuity.

Rimmer, Robert H., ed. *Adventures in Loving* (New York: New American Library, 1973). Collection of personal narratives supportive of the sexual revolution.

Rogers, Carl. *Becoming Partners* (New York: Delacorte Press, 1972). A range of interviews revealing alternative forms of partnership from inside.

Rose, Phyllis. *Parallel Lives: Five Victorian Marriages.* (New York: Vintage Books, 1984). Pitfalls of domestic life for five well-known couples revealing "the durability of the pair in all its variations."

Satir, Virginia. *People-Making* (Palo Alto, CA: Science and Behavior Books, 1972). Concepts of self-worth, communication, rules people use to govern feelings and behavior, and ways people relate to each other. Widely used as text.

Scanzoni, John. *Sexual Bargaining: Power Politics in the American Marriage* (Chicago: University of Chicago Press, 1970). Notes move of marriage toward role-equality.

Scarf, Maggie. *Intimate Partners: Patterns in Love and Marriage* (New York: Random House, 1987). Reveals sources of conflict and provides method for increasing intimacy.

Sheehy, Gail *Passages: Predictable Crises of Adult Life* (New York: Bantam, 1974). Wildly popular "roadmap" of "inevitable" personality and sexual changes.

Smith, Gerald Walker, and Alice I. Phillips. *Me, and You, and Us* (New York: Peter Wyden, Inc., 1971). Forty-seven simple exercises applying communication theory to conjugal therapy.

Smith, James R. and Lynn G., eds. *Beyond Monogamy: Recent Studies of Sexual Alternatives in Marriage* (Baltimore, MD: John Hopkins University Press, 1974). Evidence of the movement toward parity and the elimination of sex roles. Sex therapy only for dysfunction.

Thatcher, Floyd and Margaret. *Long-Term Marriage: A Search for the Ingredients of a Lifetime Partnership* (Waco, Texas: Word Books, 1981). Dozens of interviews with couples married more than 20 years: authenticity (be oneself), openness (explore together), caring (give room to grow), faith (good intentions of other), confidence (in process). communication skills, methods of handling conflict, effect of kids, midlife transition.

## Historical Studies

Gies, Frances and Joseph. *Marriage and the Family in the Middle Ages* (New York: Harper & Row, 1987). Massive scholarly historical work.

Stone, Lawrence. *The Family, Sex and Marriage: In England 1500-1800*, abridged ed. (New York: Harper Torchbooks, 1979). Places the beginning of affective individualism and companionate marriage from 1640 to 1800.

Veyne, Paul, ed. *A History of Private Life: From Pagan Rome to Byzantium,* tr. Arthur Goldhammer (Cambridge, MA: Harvard University Press, 1987). Massive scholarly work, well-written.

## C. Spiritual Coupledom

Achtemeier, Elizabeth. *The Committed Marriage* (Philadelphia: Westminster Press, 1976). The conjugal task is working together for realization, contentment, security, self-revelation.

Bethards, Betty. *Sex and Psychic Energy* (Novato, CA: Inner Light Foundation, 1977). Popularized tantra with a conventional moral stance and Raggedy-Anne illustrations.

Bird, Joseph W. and Lois F. *Freedom of Sexual Love* (New York: Doubleday, 1967). The marital embrace as a glimpse of the beatific vision, mirror of Trinity. *Marriage is for Grown-ups* (Garden City, NY: Doubleday/Image, 1971). Sex as spiritual encounter, act of virtue, means of glorifying God; a channel of grace through which couple finds Christ; a means, like prayer, for the increase of charity. *How to Make Your Wife Your Mistress* (New York: Bantam, 1972). What, when, where, how, ending with "101 Ways" and "testing your LQ (lover's quotient)." *Sexual Loving: The Experience of Love* (Garden City, NY: Doubleday, 1976). Notes inverse relationship between social involvement with others and fulfillment in marriage.

Bulka, Reuven P. *Jewish Marriage: A Halakhic Ethic* (Hoboken, NJ: KTAV Publishing House, 1986). Conservative guidebook with bibliography of classical forms dispersed throughout.

Campbell, Susan. *The Couple's Journey: Intimacy as a Path to Wholeness* (San Luis Obispo, CA: Impact Publishers, 1980). Americanized tantra with abstract illustrations.

Cotter, Jim. *Prayer at Night: A Book for the Darkness* (Exeter: Cairns Publications, 1988). Lyrical evocation of bodies as good.

Delany, Seldon P. *Married Saints* (Westminster, MD: The Newman Press, 1950). Dispels the notion that marriage is incompatible with recognized sanctity, but studies the individual rather than the couple, and gives little notion of what the ordinary, slow accumulation of heroic virtue in the conjugal state might be like. No models for conjugal sanctity, even with the inclusion of some "not yet canonized."

Demarest, Don, Jerry and Marilyn Sexton. *Marriage Encounter: A Guide for Sharing* (St. Paul: Carillon Books, 1977). Description of the weekend experience and its philosophy.

Dominian, Jack. *Marriage, Faith and Love: A Basic Guide to Christian Marriage* (New York: Crossroad, 1982). Encyclopedic survey. Permanent covenant relationship with love requires continuity, reliability, predictability. Biblical passages for life-phases: Advent (courtship), Lent (early years), Pentecost (middle years).

Emery, Pierre-Yves, *Prayer at the Heart of Life*, trans. William J. Nottingham (Maryknoll, NY: Orbis Books, 1975). Swiss Protestant brother of Taizé, who specializes in conjugal counselling. Chapter 6: "The prayer of married couples." The only theologian, to my knowledge, to have addressed this topic from a practical point of view.

Ford, Edward E. and Steven Englund. *Permanent Love: Practical Steps to a Lasting Partnership* (Minneapolis: Winston Press, 1979). A reality therapy approach to caring, with four practical steps: activity together, individual activity, verbal communication, and working out difficulties. Last chapter applies the model to relations with God and the Church.

Fromm, Erich. *The Art of Loving* (New York: Harper & Row, 1956, 1967). The only full self-transcendence is in interpersonal union with another in love (vs. orgiastic states of sex, trance, drugs which are intense, violent, occur in total being, but are transitory and periodical; and conformity with group, which is permanent, but of a sameness rather than a oneness; and creative activity, which is not interpersonal).

Gallagher, Charles A. et al. *Embodied in Love: Sacramental Spirituality and Sexual Intimacy: A New Catholic Guide to Marriage* (New York: Crossroads, 1983). Spirituality of married life stemming from the Roman Catholic Marriage Encounter movement: marriage as Trinitarian community building the body of Christ, infidelity as the decline of passion, discipline as deliberate cultivation of sexual intimacy and total awareness of other as a desired being.

Guggenbuhl-Craig, Adolf. *Marriage Dead or Alive* (Zurich: Spring Publications, 1977). Marriage is a lifelong dialectical encounter between two partners, special path for discovering soul, absence of avenues for escape. Reserved for those especially gifted in finding their salvation in intensive, continuous relationship and dialectical encounter.

Jessey, Cornelia and Irving Sussman. *Spiritual Partners: Profiles in Creative Marriage* (New York: Crossroad Press, 1982). The stuff of which saints' lives are made: biographies of Bubers, Maritains, Chestertons, Joyces, Clemens, Ward/Sheed, couples who combine romance and achievement.

Kelsey, Morton T. and Barbara. *Sacrament of Sexuality: The Spirituality and Psychology of Sex* (Warwick NY: Amity House, 1986). Biological and cultural formation of sex. Masculine and feminine sexuality, the patriarchal put-down, scripture and sexuality, and the spirituality of love.

Lewis, C. S. *A Grief Observed* (London: Faber & Faber, 1961). Journal kept after the death of his wife, Joy Davidman, reflecting on his feelings and their short but stunning marriage.

Mace, David & Vera. *Marriage East and West* (Garden City, NY: Doubleday, 1959). Quaker marriage counsellors who subsequently wrote many other books on marriage as vocation (1968), readings for couples (1985) and the sexual revolution (1970).

McCorckle, Locke. *How to Make Love: The Spiritual Nature of Sex* (New York: Grove Press, 1969; Evergreen/Black Cat, 1970). Small, helpful, nontechnical work (meditation before, gather attention with massage).

Oppenheimer, Helen. "Two Shall Become One," in Ann Belford Ulanov et al., *Men and Women: Sexual Ethics in Turbulent Times* (Cambridge, MA: Cowley Publications, 1989). The nature of marriage calls for "union" of individuals becoming more themselves; need for right metaphor and analogy; subordination of relation to kids or society is a mistake.

Ott, Gene and Mary Lou. "Couple Prayer" (interviewed by Betty and Art Winter) in *Praying*, No. 5 (P.O. Box 419335, Kansas City, MO 64141). A new reality, like a third self, comes into being.

Pelz, Werner and Lotte. *God Is No More* (London: Victor Gallancz Ltd., 1963). Pleasant essays on marriage as training in gracefulness and spontaneity.

Rousseau, Mary, & Charles Gallagher. *Sex is Holy* (Rockport, MA: Element, Inc., 1986). Sex as prayer, from the head of Marriage Encounter and a professor of philosophy.

Ryan, Kevin and Marilyn. *Making a Marriage: A Personal Book of Love, Marriage and Family* (New York: St. Martin's Press, 1982). The biography of a marriage, three voices, each with its own typeface, plus distilled advice on flash points, skills needed, strategies for dealing with anger.

Schachter, Zalman. *The First Step: A Guide for the New Jewish Spirit* (New York: Bantam, 1983). Engaging ideas for nurturing the mammal, the mensch, and the marriage.

Valentini, Norberto and Clara di Meglio. *Sex and the Confessional*, tr. Melton S. Davis (New York: Stein and Day, 1975). Portions of 636 confessions, collected on tape and based on characteristic situations worked out beforehand.

Vanauken, Sheldon. *A Severe Mercy* (New York: Bantam, 1977). Biography of a marriage showing the perils of traditional spirituality.

Welwood, John, ed. *Challenge of the Heart: Love, Sex, and Intimacy in Changing Times* (Boston: Shambala, 1985). Superb collection of short provocative writings on all aspects of eros, marred only by categorical exclusion of homosexuals. *Journey of the Heart: Intimate Relationship and the Path of Love* (New York: Harper/Perennial, 1990). Spiritual self-help from a clinical psychologist and psychotherapist.

Wilkes, Paul. "A Monk is Not Manqué in the Bosom of His Family," in the *National Catholic Reporter* (Feb. 19, 1988), p. 1. Ex-Trappist reinterprets ascetic discipline.

## D. Sexuality

Alexandrian. *Les Libérateurs de l'amour* (Paris: Éditions du Seuil, 1977). A mine of information on explorers of love's boundaries on all sides. Sees the 20th century as a unique attempt to synthesize exclusive love and libertinage.

Alman, Isadora. *Aural Sex and Verbal Intercourse* (Burlingame, CA: Down There Press, 1984). Reports from the San Francisco Sex Information hotline.

*Ananga Ranga* ["Stage of the Love God"], (London: Collins/Fount, 1978). 16th-century classic on mysticism and religion, how the married can lead life in union, as with 32 partners (positions).

Avalon, Arthur (Sir John Woodroffe). *The Serpent Power: Introduction to Tantrism* (Madras: Ganesh et Cie., 1950). Early work introducing Kundalini Yoga to the West.

Barbach, Lonnie Garfield. *For Yourself: The Fulfillment of Female Sexuality* (New York: New American Library, 1975). Step-by-step program for pre-orgasmic women. *For Each Other: Sharing Sexual Intimacy* (New York: New American Library, 1982). Guide for women who want more joyful sexual relations.

Chang, Jolan. *The Tao of Love and Sex: The Ancient Chinese Way to Ecstasy* (New York: Dutton, 1977). Personal exposition of Chinese sexology, written mainly for men. Contains classical lists of signs for recognizing female satisfaction, kinds of penile thrust, and colorful names for vaginas of different depths and for various love positions.

Chia, Mantak and Michael Winn. *Taoist Secrets of Love: Cultivating Male Sexual Energy* (Santa Fe, NM: Aurora Press, 1984). Program focused on increasing male sexual energy, by a Thai expert on natural healing. In the Kundalini and Taoist Yoga traditions, it combines Western anatomical terminology with Eastern poetic designations. Technical and illustrative line drawings.

Chia, Mantak & Maneewan. *Healing Love through the Tao: Cultivating Female Sexual Energy* (Huntington, NY: Healing Tao Books, 1986). Parallel course for women, written with his wife, a medical technician and dietician.

Crooks, Robert, and Karla Baur. *Our Sexuality* (Menlo Park, CA: The Benjamin/Cummings Publishing Company, 1980). Good standard work.

D'Emilio, John and Estelle B. Freedman. *Intimate Matters: A History of Sexuality in America* (New York: Harper & Row, 1988). Fascinating scholarly chronicle of sexual mores from 1600 on, including Indians, blacks, the free love movement of the late 19th century, and Kellogg and Graham's famous foods developed in the hope of substituting for the disappearing control of sexuality by the family.

Douglas, Nik and Penny Slinger. *Sexual Secrets: The Alchemy of Ecstasy* (Rochester, VT: Destiny Books, 1979). Study of the great cultures of the East by a writer and an artist familiar with the traditions. Included, newly translated, are the *Kama Sutra, Ananga Ranga*, drawings of some of the finest Tantric art (never before published), and the major Taoist love treatises.

Flandrin, Jean-Louis. *Le Sexe et l'Occident: Évolution des attitudes et des comportements* (Paris: Éditions du Seuil, 1981). Examination of the cultural role in forming attitudes toward sexuality.

Gordan, David Cole. *Self-Love* (New York: Macmillan, 1970). Apology for solitary cultivation of sex.

Gordan, Elaine. *Intimate Terms* (New York: Zebra, 1990). Good suggestion for solving the problem of sex talk.

Hunt, Morton M. *The Natural History of Love* (New York: Grove Press, 1959). Condensation of an enormous amount of literature on sex, courtship, marriage, romance, and marital status.

"J." *The Sensuous Woman* (New York: Dell Publishing Company, 1969). Early and sensational book of exercises and suggestions for enhancing sexual experience. Some misinformation.

*The Kama Sutra of Vatsyayana* ("Aphorisms on Love"), tr. Sir Richard Burton and F. F. Arbuthnot (London: Unwin Paperbacks, 1981). Victorian translation of Hindu classic on the art and science of love, pleasure, and sensual gratification. Householder's instructions on sexual technique, no mystical idea of union with the deity.

*Koka Shastra, being the Ratirahasiya of Kokkoka, and Other Medieval Indian Writings on Love*, tr. Alex Comfort (Boston: Unwin Paperbacks, 1982). 12th-century classic, more detail than the *Kama Sutra*.

LaHaye, Tim and Beverly. *The Act of Marriage: The Beauty of Sexual Love* (Grand Rapids, MI: Zondervan, 1976). Advice on sexual adjustment from the president of Family Life Seminars.

Masters, William H. and Virginia E. Johnson. *The Pleasure Bond: A New Look at Sexuality and Commitment* (New York: Bantam Books, 1976). Preventive medicine for sexual dysfunction and an apology for commitment.

Okada, Hideko. "The Sexual Ritual in a Messianic Religion," presented at the Inner Asia Colloquium at the University of Washington in Seattle, 5 April, 1971. First work to bring *The Yellow Book (Tung Chen Huang Shu)* and its commentary to scholarly tradition.

Saraswati, Sunyata and Bodhi Avinasha. *Jewel in the Lotus: The Sexual Path to Higher Consciousness* (San Francisco: Kriya Jyoti Tantra Society, 1987). "A complete and systematic course in Tantric Kriya Yoga," with line drawings and glossary, each lesson followed by suggestions for individual practice, couple practice, and awareness, the last chapter describing the sacred *maithuna* rite.

Singer, June. *Androgyny: Toward A New Theory of Sexuality* (Garden City, NY: Anchor/Doubleday, 1976). The tradition and interpretation for all sorts and conditions today by a Jungian psychologist. *Energies of Love: Sexuality Re-visioned* (Garden City, NY: Anchor/Doubleday, 1983). Transpersonal psychological perspective.

Skolnick, Arlene S. *The Intimate Environment: Exploring Marriage and the Family* (Boston: Little, Brown and Company, 1983). Widely used, easily readable text with chapters on gender, love, and marriage, summarizing cross-cultural and other research.

Stevens, John O. *Awareness: Exploring, Experimenting, Experiencing* (New York: Bantam Books, 1976). Very thorough study with many practical exercises.

Tannahill, Reay. *Sex in History* (London: Hamish Hamilton, 1980). History of the ways sexuality has influenced the course of human progress from pre-history through the present.

Van Gulik, Robert. *Sexual Life in Ancient China: A Preliminary Survey of Chinese Sex and Society from ca 1500 B.C. till 1644 A.D.* (Leiden: E. J. Brill, 1961). Scholarly but very readable work by Dutch diplomat, whose wife was Chinese.

Zilbergeld, Bernie. *Male Sexuality* (New York: Bantam Books, 1978). Warm-hearted examinations of myths, physical aspects, and problem areas of the sexual life for men. Very practical.

# Endnotes

## Chapter 1: "Spirituality" is Celibate

1. *The Westminster Dictionary of Christian Spirituality* (Philadelphia: The Westminster Press, 1983).

2. Ernest Boyer, Jr., "Edges and Rhythms," in *Sojourners* 11:6 (June 1982), p. 14.

3. Helen Waddell, *The Desert Fathers* (Ann Arbor, MI: University of Michigan Press, 1957), p. 112.

4. Ibid., p. 119.

5. Ibid., p. 112.

6. Ibid., p. 67.

7. Ibid., p. 99.

8. Mary Anne McPherson Oliver, "Taizé and Contemplation: a Personal Approach," *Studia Mystica* II/1 (Spring, 1979), p. 7.

9. *The Rule of Saint Benedict* (Garden City, NY: Doubleday/Image, 1975), p. 94.

10. *Rule*, p. 47.

11. William Johnston, *The Still Point: Reflections on Zen and Christian Mysticism* (New York: Harper & Row, 1970), and *Silent Music: the Science of Meditation* (New York, Harper & Row, 1974).

12. Jacques Ellul, *Prayer and Modern Man* (New York: Seabury, 1970).

13. Alan Jones, *Soul Making: The Desert Way of Spirituality* (San Francisco: Harper & Row, 1985).

14. E. Glenn Hinson, *A Serious Call to a Contemplative Lifestyle* (Philadelphia: Westminster Press, 1974).

15. Elizabeth O'Connor, *Call to Commitment* (New York: Harper & Row, 1963), and *Search for Silence* (Waco, TX: Word Books, 1972).

16. U. T. Holmes III, *The History of Christian Spirituality: An Analytical Introduction* (New York: Seabury Press, 1980).

17. Donald Goergan, *The Sexual Celibate* (Garden City, NY: Doubleday/Image, 1979), p. 57.

18. Paul Evdokimov, *Le sacrement de l'amour à la lumière de la tradition orthodoxe* (Paris: Editions de l'Épi, 1962), p. 243. This is available in English, *The Sacrament of Love: The Conjugal Mystery in the Light of the Orthodox Tradition,* tr. Anthony P. Gythiel and Victoria Steadman (Crestwood, NY: St. Vladimir's Seminary Press, 1985).

19. Charles M. Olson, "The Closet, the House and the Sanctuary," *Christian Century* (9 December 1981), 98: 1285–1289.

20. Boyer, pp. 16-17. Cf. also *A Way in the World: Family Life as Spiritual Discipline* (San Francisco: Harper & Row, 1984), reissued in 1988 as *Finding God at Home: Family Life as Spiritual Discipline.*

21. Geoffrey Parrinder, *Sex in the World's Religions* (London: Sheldon Press, 1980), p. 191.

22. Kenneth E. Kirk, *The Vision of God: The Christian Doctrine of the Summum Bonum* (New York: Harper & Row, 1966), p. 186.

23. See David G. Hunter, *Marriage in the Early Church* (Minneapolis, MN: Augsburg Fortress, 1992), pp. 41-56.

24. Pierre Riché, *La vie quotidienne dans l'empire carolingien* (Paris, 1973), p. 65.

25. Basil, *The Fathers of the Church: A New Translation*, tr. Sister Agnes Clare Way (New York: Fathers of the Church, Inc., 1951), v. 13, letter #22.

26. Basil, v. 9, "Long Rules."

27. Thomas Becon, cited in D(errick) S(herwin) Bailey, *The Sexual Relation in Christian Thought* (New York: Harper & Row, 1959), p. 103.

28. Parrinder, p. 231.

29. Parrinder, p. 23.

30. Kenneth Stevenson, *Nuptial Blessing: A Study of Christian Marriage Rites* (London: Alcuin Club/SPCK, 1982), p. 67.

31. Edmund Leites, *The Puritan Conscience and Modern Sexuality* (New Haven: Yale University Press, 1986), p. 12.

32. *Papal Teachings: Matrimony,* by the Benedictine monks of Solesmes (Boston: St. Paul Editions, 1963).

33. Pierre Delooz, *Sociologie et Canonisations* (La Haye: Martinus Nihoff, 1969).

34. Lawrence Cunningham, *The Meaning of Saints* (San Francisco: Harper & Row, 1980).

35. John R. H. Moorman, *The Anglican Spiritual Tradition* (Springfield, IL: Templegate Publishers, 1983), pp. 44-53.

36. "Mariage," in *Dictionnaire de Théologie Catholique*, eds. A. Vacant, E. Mangenot, E. Amann (Paris: Letouzey & Ané, 1927), 9:2180-2181.

37. Roland H. Bainton, *The Reformation of the Sixteenth Century* (Boston: Beacon, 1952), p. 255.

38. John Kent, "Problems of a Protestant Spirituality," in *The London Quarterly Review* (Jan. 1966), pp. 28-33.

39. Evdokimov, p. 243.

40. Gerald G. May, *Care of Mind, Care of Spirit: Psychiatric Dimensions of Spiritual Direction* (San Francisco: Harper & Row, 1982), p. 29.

41. Elizabeth Rice Achtemeier, *The Committed Marriage* (Philadelphia: Westminster, 1976), p. 163.

42. William A. Barry and William J. Connolly, *The Practice of Spiritual Direction* (New York: Seabury Press, 1983), pp. 3-7.

43. Anne Fremantle, *Woman's Way to God* (New York, St. Martin's Press, 1977), p. 105.

## Chapter 2: Conjugal Spirituality

1. Scott Peck, *The Road Less Travelled: A New Psychology of Loves, Traditional Values and Spiritual Growth* (New York: Simon & Schuster/Touchstone, 1978), p. 161.

2. "Sexuality," by Daniel Didomizio, in *The Westminster Dictionary of Spirituality,* ed. Gordon S. Wakefield (Philadelphia: The Westminster Press, 1983), pp. 353-354.

3. *De divisionibus Naturae,* II,4; II,8,12,14, cited in Julius Evola, *The Metaphysics of Sex* (London: East-West Publications, 1983), p. 180.

4. Mircea Eliade, *The Two and the One* (London: Harvill Press, 1962), p. 104.

5. Cf. William Johnston's discussion of "Mystical friendship," in *Silent Music: The Science of Meditation* (New York: Harper & Row, 1974), pp. 149-159.

6. (A monk of the Eastern Church), *Orthodox Spirituality: An Outline of the Orthodox Ascetical and Mystical Tradition,* 2nd ed. (Crestwood, NY: Saint Vladimir's Seminary Press, 1978), pp. 93, 106.

7. Vladimir Sergeiev Soloviev, *The Meaning of Love,* trans. Jane Marshall (London: Geoffrey Bles, The Centenary Press, 1945). For the genesis of Soloviev's teaching on love, see D. Strémooukhoff, *Vladimir Soloviev and His Messianic Work,* trans. Elizabeth Meyendorff, ed. Phillip Guilbeau and Heather Elise MacGregor (Belmont, MA: Nordland Publ., 1980), pp. 306-8.

8. Geoffrey Parrinder, *Sex in the World's Religions* (London, Sheldon Press, 1980), p. 191.

9. Martin Buber, *I and Thou,* tr. Walter Kaufmann (New York: Charles Scribner's Sons, 1970), p. 69.

10. For a good introduction, see Don Demarest, Jerry & Marilyn Sexton, *Marriage Encounter: A Guide for Sharing* (St. Paul: Carillon Books, 1977).

11. Paul Evdokimov, *The Sacrament of Love: The Conjugal Mystery in the Light of the Orthodox Tradition,* tr. Anthony P. Gythiel and Victoria Steadman (Crestwood, NY: St. Vladimir's Seminary Press, 1985).

12. Joseph and Lois Bird, *Freedom of Sexual Love* (Garden City, NY: Doubleday, 1967), and *Marriage is for Grown-ups* (Garden City, NY: Doubleday, 1971).

13. For a short resumé see Geoffrey Parrinder, *Sex in the World's Religions* (London: Sheldon Press, 1980), pp. 202-239. Bailey's and Schillebeeckx's works, though early, are still indispensable. For a more recent and European Protestant perspective, see Eric Fuchs, *Sexual Desire and Love: Origins and History of the Christian Ethic of Sexuality and Marriage,* trans. Marsha Daigle (New York: Seabury Press, 1983).

14. An early example is David and Vera Mace's *Marriage East and West* (Garden City, NY: Doubleday, 1959). Sample works from other decades include Judson T. and Mary G. Landis, *Building a Successful Marriage* (Englewood Cliffs, NJ: Prentice-Hall, 1973), Howard J. and Charlotte H. Clinebell, *Intimate Marriage* (New York: Harper and Row, 1970), and Wallace and Juanita Holt Denton, *Creative Couples: The Growth Factor in Marriage* (Philadelphia: Westminster Press, 1983).

15. Erich Fromm, *The Art of Loving* (New York: Harper and Row, 1956), for example.

16. Robert O. Blood, Jr. and Donald M. Wolfe, *Husbands and Wives: The Dynamics of Married Living* (New York: The Free Press, 1960) and Floyd and Margaret Thatcher, *Long-Term Marriage: A Search for the Ingredients of a Lifetime Partnership* (Waco, TX: Word Books, 1981).

17. William Basset, *The Bond of Marriage: An Ecumenical and Interdisciplinary Study* (Notre Dame [IN]: University of Notre Dame Press, 1968).

18. Paul Avis, *Eros and the Sacred* (Harrisburg, PA: Morehouse Publishing, 1990), pp. 125-126.

19. Margharita Laski, *Ecstasy: A Study of Some Secular and Religious Experiences* (Bloomington: Indiana University Press, 1962).

20. Geoffrey Parrinder, *Mysticism in the World Religions* (New York: Oxford University Press, 1976), p. 191.

21. Cf. Maurice Nédoncelle's discussion in *God's Encounter with Man: A Contemporary Approach to Prayer*, tr. A. Manson (New York: Sheed & Ward, 1964), and Parrinder's, *Mysticism in the World Religions*, p. 191.

22. William James, *The Varieties of Religious Experience* (New York: The New American Library, 1958), p. 164.

23. William Johnston, *The Still Point: Reflections on Zen and Christian Mysticism* (New York: Harper & Row, 1970), pp. 36-37.

24. Herbert Slade, *Exploration into Contemplative Prayer* (New York: Paulist Press, 1975), p. 132.

25. Goergan, p. 12.

## Chapter 3: The Human Phenomenon: Coupledom

1. "Marriage," in *The Encyclopedia Britannica* (Chicago: William Benton Publisher, 1964).

2. William Blackstone, *Commentaries,* ed. William Carey Jones (San Francisco: Bancroft-Whitney Co., 1916), Vol. I, pp. 625–634.

3. John L. McKenzie, "Aspects of Old Testament Thought," in *The Jerome Bible Commentary*, eds. Raymond E. Brown, Joseph A. Fitzmyer, and Roland E. Murphy (Englewood Cliffs, NJ: Prentice-Hall, 1968), 77:68.

4. Gene and Mary Lou Ott, "Couple Prayer: When Two Become One and Three," interview by Betty and Art Winter, in *Praying*, No. 5, p. 27.

5. Betty Bethards, *Sex and Psychic Energy* (Novato, CA: Inner Light Foundation, 1977), p. 69.

6. Lederer, William J. and Don D. Jackson, *The Mirages of Marriage* (New York: W. W. Norton & Co., 1968), p. 130.

7. Gail Sheehy, *Passages: Predictable Crises of Adult Life* (New York: Bantam Books, Inc., 1977), pp. 445-446.

8. Peter Berger and Hansfried Kellner, "Marriage and the Construction of Reality: An Exercise in the Microsociology of Knowledge," reprint from *Diogenes* (1964), 46:1-25.

9. Jean Rostand, *Le mariage: notes et maximes* (Paris: Hachette, 1964), p. 77.

10. Penelope Washbourn, *On Becoming Woman: The Quest for Wholeness in Female Experience* (New York: Harper & Row, 1977), p. 91.

11. Washbourn, pp. 35-49.

12. Charles WilliaMA, *Descent into Hell* (Grand Rapids, Mich: Eerdmans, 1949), p. 130.

13. Maria Hippius, quoted in Karlfried Graf Dürckheim, *Méditer: pourquoi et comment*, trans. Catherine de Bose (Paris: Le Courrier du Livre, 1976), p. 26.

14. Cf. Mary McDermott Shideler, *The Theology of Romantic Love: A Study in the Writings of Charles Williams* (New York: Harper and Brothers, 1962).

15. Arthur N. Schwartz, Cherie L. Snyder, and James A. Peterson, *Aging and Life: an Introduction to Gerontology* (New York: Holt, Rinehart & Winston, 1984), pp. 223-226.

16. J. V. Cunningham, *The Collected Poems and Epigrams* (Chicago: Swallow Press, 1971), p. 124.

17. W. B. Yeats, "Among School Children," in *The Collected Poems* (New York: Macmillan Pub. Co., 1954), p. 214.

## Chapter 4: The Spiritual Phenomenon: Henosis

1. Joseph and Lois Bird, *Sexual Living: The Experience of Love* (New York: Doubleday, 1976), p. 199.

2. *The Confessions of St. Augustine*, trans. John K. Ryan (New York: Doubleday/Image Book, 1960), Bk. 4, ch. 6.

3. Gregory of Nazianzen, as quoted in Francis de Sales' *Introduction to the Devout Life*, trans. & ed. John K. Ryan (New York: Harper Bros, 1949), ch. 18.

4. J. Aumann, "Contemplation," in *The New Catholic Encyclopedia* (San Francisco, 1967), 4:258–263.

5. Paul Evdokimov, "Conjugal Priesthood," trans. Agnes Cunningham, in *Marriage and Christian Tradition* by George Crespy, Paul Evdokimov, and Christian Duquoc (Techny, IL: Divine Word Pubs., 1968), p. 69.

6. Maurice Nédoncelle, *Love and the Person*, tr. Sister Ruth Adelaide (New York: Sheed & Ward, 1966), pp. 124-133.

7. Ruthellen Josselson, *The Space Between Us: Exploring the Dimensions of Human Relationships* (San Francisco: Jossey-Bass Publishers, 1992).

8. Dürckheim, *Méditieren*, p. 83.

9. Alexander Yelchaninov, "Fragments of a Diary: 1881-1934," in *A Treasury of Russian Spirituality* ed. G. P. Fédotov (New York: Harper & Row, 1965), p. 446.

10. Julius Evola, *The Metaphysics of Sex* (London: East–West Publications, 1983), p.2.

## Chapter 5: Stages

1. C. S. Lewis, *A Grief Observed* (London: Faber & Faber, 1961).

2. "Father Yelchaninov: The Teacher of Self-Examination," in *A Treasury of Russian Spirituality*, ed. G. P. Fédotov (New York: Harper Torchbooks, Harper & Row, 1965), pp. 429, 446, 470, 474, 476.

3. D[errick] S[herwin] Bailey, *The Man-Woman Relation in Christian Thought* (London: Longmans, 1959), p. 276.

4. Joseph W. Bird and Lois F. Bird, *The Freedom of Sexual Love* (Garden City, NY: Doubleday/Image, 1967), p. 51.

5. Bird, p. 149

6. Maillot, *Vocabulaire biblique,* s.v. "Prière," quoted in Jacques Ellul, *Prayer and the Modern Man,* tr. Edward Hopkins (New York: Seabury Press, 1973), p. 56.

7. Katherine Anne Porter, "Marriage is Belonging," in *Collected Essays and Occasional Writings of Katherine Anne Porter* (New York: Delacorte Press, 1970), p. 187.

8. Sidney Callahan, quoted in Letha Scanzoni and Nancy Hardesty, *All We're Meant to Be* (Nashville: Abingdon, 1974), p. 190.

9. John Welwood, ed., *Challenge of the Heart: Love, Sex and Intimacy in Changing Times* (Boston: Shambala, 1985), p. 154.

10. William Johnston, *Silent Music: The Science of Meditation* (New York: Harper/Perennial Lib., 1974), p. 21.

11. Dyckman, Katherine Marie, and L. Patrick Carroll, *Inviting the Mystic Supporting the Prophet: An Introduction to Spiritual Direction* (New York: Paulist Press, 1981), pp. 45-46.

12. Herbert Slade, *Exploration into Contemplative Prayer* (New York: Paulist Press, 1975), p. 64.

13. Betty Bethards, *Sex and Psychic Energy* (Novato, CA: Inner Light Foundation, 1977), p. 91.

14. Elmer E. and A.M. Green, "On the Meaning of Transpersonal: Some Metaphysical Perspectives," in the *Journal of Transpersonal Psychology,* No. 1, 1971, pp. 27-47.

15. Carla Needleman, "Falling Toward Grace," in *Studia Mystica* V, 1 (Spring 1982), p. 50.

16. Monford Harris, "Marriage as Metaphysics: A Study of the *'Iggereth-Hakodesh,"* in the *Hebrew Union College Annual* (vol. 33, 1962), p. 201.

17. *The Holy Letter: A Study in Medieval Jewish Sexual Morality,* ed. & tr. Seymour J. Cohen (New York: KTAV Pub. House, 1976), p. 28.

18. Moses ben Nachman, mentioned in Israel Mattuck's *Jewish Ethics* (London: Hutchinson House, 1953), p. 137.

19. *Keth.* 5.6; R. Eliezer, in H[erbert] Danby, *The Mishnah* (Oxford, 1933), p. 252.

20. Keth., ibid.

21. Donald Goergan, *The Sexual Celibate* (Garden City, NY: Doubleday, 1979), p. 43.

22. Phyllis Trible, *God and the Rhetoric of Sexuality* (Philadelphia: Fortress Press, 1078), p. 93.

23. *Holy Letter,* p. 50.

24. Paul Evdokimov, *Le Sacrement de l'Amour: le mystère conjugale à la lumière de la tradition orthodoxe* (Paris: Éditions de l'Épi, 1962), p. 243. The

English translation is *The Sacrament of Love: The Nuptial Mystery in the Light of Orthodox Tradition* (Crestwood, NY: St. Vladimir's Seminary Press, 1985).

25. John Ruysbroeck, *The Book of Supreme Truth*, X, quoted in Patrick Grant's *The Literature of Mysticism in Western Tradition* (London: Macmillan Press, 1983), p. 48.

26. See my discussion in "Conjugal Spirituality (or Radical Proximity): A New Form of Con-templ-ation," *Spirituality Today* Vol. 43, No. 1 (Spring 1991), pp. 53-67.

27. Augustin Poulain, "Ecstasy," in *The Catholic Encyclopedia* (New York: Appleton, 1907-1922).

28. Bird, pp. 27, 149.

29. Bird, p. 145.

30. Andrew M. Greeley, *Sexual Intimacy* (New York: Seabury/Crossroad, 1973), p. 198.

31. Bird, p. 148.

32. Elizabeth Achtemeier, *The Committed Marriage* (Philadelphia: Westminster, 1976), p. 163.

33. Albert Dessesprit, *Le mariage un sacrement* (Paris: Le Centurion, 1981), p. 69.

34. Augustine, *Confessions* (IX, 10), tr. R.S. Pine-Coffin (Baltimore: Penguin, 1962), p. 197.

35. Cf. my discussion in "Mystical Experience and the Literary Technique of Silence," *Studia Mystica* I, 2 (Spring 1978), pp. 1011.

36. "The Dark Night of the Soul," in *The Collected Works of St. John of the Cross* (I, 4), tr. Kieran Kavanaugh and Otilio Rodriguez (Washington, DC: Institute of Carmelite Studies, 1973), pp. 303-304.

37. Maximus the Confessor, quoted in "Conjugal Priesthood," by Paul Evdokimov, in George Crespy, Paul Evdokimov, and Christian Duquoc, *Marriage and the Christian Tradition*, tr. Sister Agnes Cunningham, SSCM (Techny, IL: Divine Word Publications, 1968), p. 88.

38. Thomas Merton, *Seeds of Contemplation* (New York: Dell, 1959), pp. 109, 120.

39. Maurice Nédoncelle, *God's Encounter with Man: A Contemporary Approach to Prayer* (New York: Random House/Vintage, 1970), pp. 148, 205.

40. Johnston, *Silent Music,* pp. 153-154.

41. William Johnston, *The Inner Eye of Love: Mysticism and Religion* (London: Fount Paperbacks, 1981 [first published in the USA by Harper & Row, Inc., in 1978]), p. 19.

42. William Johnston, *The Mirror Mind* (San Francisco: Harper & Row, 1981), p. 124.

43. John Cotter, *Prayer at Night* (Exeter: Cairns Pub., 1988), p. 62.

44. Bird, p. 150.

45. *Serm. 1.4*, quoted in "The Practice of Christian Life: the Birth of the Laity," by Jacques Fontaine, in *Christian Spirituality: Origins to the Twelfth Cen-*

*tury,* ed. Bernard McGinn and John Meyendorff, in collaboration with Jean Leclercq (New York: Crossroad, 1985), p. 453.

46. Rosemary Haughton, *Theology of Marriage* (Butler, WI: Clergy Book Service, 1971), p. 47.

47. Alan Watts, *Nature Man, and Woman* (New York: Random House/Vintage, 1970), pp. 148, 205.

48. Johnston, *The Inner Eye,* p. 19.

49. Vladimir Sergeevich Soloviev, *The Meaning of Love,* tr. Jane Marshall (London: Geoffrey Bles/The Centenary Press, 1945), pp. 25-29. Cf. also D. Strémooukhoff, *Vladimir Soloviev and His Messianic Work,* tr. Elizabeth Meyendorff, ed. Phillip Guilbeau and Heather Elise MacGregor (Belmont, MA: Nordland Publishing Company, 1980), p. 311.

50. Evdokimov, *Sacrament of Love,* pp. 162-163.

51. D(errick) S(herwin) Bailey, *The Mystery of Love and Marriage: A Study in the Theology of Sexual Relation* (New York: Harper & Bros., 1952).

52. Watts, p. 205.

53. James B. Nelson, *Embodiment: An Approach to Sexuality and Christian Theology* (Minneapolis, Minnesota: Augsburg Publishing House, 1978), p. 255ff; U(rban) T(igner) Holmes, *Spirituality for Ministry* (San Francisco: Harper & Row, 1982), pp. 95-112; and Bailey, *op. cit.*

54. Julius Evola, *The Metaphysics of Sex* (London: East-West Publications, 1983), p. 139.

55. Charles A. Gallagher, George A. Maloney, Mary F. Rousseau and Paul F. Wilczak, *Embodied in Love: Sacramental Spirituality and Sexual Intimacy* (New York: Crossroad, 1983), p. 12.

56. *The Autobiography of St. Teresa of Avila: The Life of Teresa of Jesus,* tr. and ed. E. Allison Peers from the crit. ed. of P. Silverio de Santa Teresa (Garden City, NY: Image/Doubleday, 1960), pp. 274-275.

57. Quoted in Geoffrey Parrinder, *Sex in the World's Religions* (London: Sheldon Press, 1980), p. 189.

58. Johnston, *The Mirror Mind,* p. 121.

59. Trible, p. 160.

## Chapter 6: Conjugal Exercise and Ritual

1. Daniel J. O'Hanlon, "Yoga as a Help for Prayer," workshop handout, 1979.

2. Sheila Kitzinger, *Women's Experience of Sex* (New York: G. P. Putnam's Sons, 1983), pp. 41-50.

3. James P. Carse, *Finite and Infinite Games: A Vision of Life as Play and Possibility* (New York: Ballantine Books, 1986), pp. 3-11.

4. Herbert Slade, *Contemplative Intimacy* (London: Darton Longman and Todd, 1977), p. 200.

5. Gail Sheehy, *Passages: Predictable Crises of Adult Life* (New York: Dutton, 1976), p. 51.

6. Paul Wilkes, "A Monk is Not Manqué in the Bosom of His Family," in the *National Catholic Reporter* (Feb. 19, 1988), p. 7.

7. "The Gospel of Philip," tr. Wesley W. Isenberg, in *The Nag Hammadi Library*, ed. James M. Robinson (San Francisco: Harper & Row, 1977), pp. 131-151.

8. "Gospel of Phillip", p. 144.

9. Ibid., p. 142.

10. Ibid., p. 150.

11. Ibid., p. 139.

12. Clement of Alexandria, *Stromateis*, 3.27ff.

13. G. G. Coulton, *Social Life in Britain from the Conquest to the Reformation* (1918), pp. 200-264.

14. Ewert H. Cousins, *Christ of the Twenty-First Century* (Rockport, MA: Element, Inc., 1992).

15. Christopher Derrick, *Sex and Sacredness: a Catholic Homage to Venus* (San Francisco, CA: Ignatius Press, 1982), pp. 67-72.

16. Slade, p. 202.

17. Stevenson, *Contemplative Intimacy*, p. 13.

18. Maurice Lamm, *The Jewish Way in Love and Marriage* (San Francisco: Harper & Row, 1980), p. 33. See also Parrinder, *Sex in the World's Religions* (London: Sheldon Press, 1980), p. 191, and J. Bonsirven, *Palestinian Judaism in the Time of Jesus Christ*, tr. William Wolf (New York: Holt, Rinehart & Winston, 1964), p. 207.

19. James A. Mohler, *The Heresy of Monasticism* (New York: Alba House, 1971), p. 34.

20. Hippolytus, *The Apostolic Tradition*, tr. Burton Scott Easton (Cambridge [Eng.]: The University Press, 1934), p. 36.

21. Ibid.

## Chapter 7

1. Tertullian, *Ad uxorem*, 2, 9 (PL, 1, 1302).

2. Martin Buber, *I and Thou*, tr. Walter Kaufmann (New York: Charles Scribner's Sons, 1970), p. 89.

3. Carl Jung, *Psychology and Religion* (New Haven: Yale University Press, 1938), p. 537.

# Name Index

Abraham, 72-73
Abraham, Abbot, 4
Abraham, St., 111
Achtemeier, Elizabeth, 18, 77, 144
Adam, 66-67, 72
Adorni, Julian, 111
Advayasiddhe, 106
Aelred of Rievaulx, 24, 64, 79, 128
Agatho, Abbot, 3
Akiba, Rabbi, 83
Alain de Lille, 24
Alexandrian, 148
Alexis, 111
Alman, Isadora, 148
Amadeus of Savoy, 115
Ambrose, 119
Andrewes, Lancelot, 14, 17
Anselm, 82, 119
Antony, 3, 87, 112, 119
Aquinas, 119
Aristotle, 135
Ars, Curé de, 119
Asclepius, 119
Association of Couples for Marriage En-
  richment, 140
Athanasius, 120
Atharveda, 120
Attwater, Donald, 114
Augustine, 46, 64, 77-78, 83, 95, 108,
  111, 119, 135, 137
Avalon, Arthur, 148
Avinasha, Bodhi, 150
Avis, Paul, 27

Bach, George R., 141
Baelz, Peter, 69, 107, 128
Bailey, D. S., 57, 82, 120, 128
Bainton, Roland, 17
Barbach, Lonnie Garfield, 148
Barbeau, Clayton C., 141

Barry, William A., 18-19
Barth, 120
Basil, 13, 46, 111, 112, 120
Bates, Marilyn, 142
Bathsheba, 62
Baur, Karla, 149
Beauvoir, Simone de, 36
Becon, Thomas, 15
Benedict, 5, 7, 9, 87
Berger, Peter, 35
Berman, Morris, 128
Bernard, 23, 120
Berry, Wendell, 74
Berzon, Betty, 141
Bethards, Betty, 55, 144
Bezabel, 72
Bird, Joseph W. and Lois F., 26, 57-58,
  76, 81-82, 144
Bharati, 120
Blackstone, William, 30
Blood, Robert O., Jr., 141
Bonaventure, 120
Bonsirven, J., 129
Boyer, Ernst, Jr., 129
Brancusi, 49, 64, 72, 92
Bridget, 114
Brown, Peter, 140
Bruckner, 120
Buber, Martin, 25, 120, 129
Bucer, 120
Bukharev, Alexander, Jr., 25
Bulka, Reuven P., 144
Bunyan, John, 17
Bynum, 121

Caesarius, 111, 121
Caffarel, Henri, 25, 129
Cady, Linell E., 129
Calvin, John, 15, 26, 121
Campbell, Susan, 55, 144

# Subject Index

166